How to Get Your Book
Published Free in Minutes
and
Marketed Worldwide
in Days

A step-by-step guide
for new or veteran publishers

Gordon Burgett

For information, contact Communication Unlimited,
P.O. Box 845, Novato, CA 94948
(800) 563-1454 / www.gordonburgett.com

First printing,
April 2010

►Cover Design by Douglas Burgett
►Proofreading by Sharon Rinderer

ISBN 9780982663516 (Bound)
ISBN 9780982663509 (Digital)

Table of Contents

How to Get Your Book Published Free in Minutes
and Marketed Worldwide in Days

Dedication

I never imagined a life publishing, writing, and speaking when I was young and bouncing from college to college and living in Brazil, Colombia, and Ecuador, then Illinois and California. But it kept following me and beckoning, and I succumbed. Mostly, I like the wordsmithing and giving long legs to teaching and sharing. There have been 100 supportive, helping friends who made that possible—too many to single out. Please know that I'm grateful, and that together we've been able to help others see their words in print, too. Thanks to every one of you.

Gordon Burgett

Legal Disclaimer

The ideas, suggestions, and advice provided in this book are those of the author. While every effort has been made to present sound and accurate legal and practical guidance, the information herein is not warranted and does not constitute legal advice. The reader should be aware that the field of publishing is in a constant state of change. Readers are strongly encouraged to check with private legal counsel before undertaking any decision that may require legal guidance or implementing or adopting any policy, procedure, or practice.

Introduction

I've stumbled, almost literally, on what may be a miracle in the publishing world. This book can help you take advantage of it immediately—and quickly make you a published author!

The miracle? If you write a book and save it in a ready-to-print file, there are seven legitimate publishers who will eagerly convert that file into a professional-looking book (within minutes, if it's an e-book, days if it's bound), then sell your book worldwide just days later.

That's right. You write and they promptly publish and market.

How much will that cost you out of pocket? Absolutely nothing. (Well, a pittance. You must pay the postage to get the bound proofs back to read them! About $20, versus $500-5,000 if you publish it yourself.) E-books are totally free.

Let me say it differently. There are first-rate publishers that produce books identical to those you see in the bookstore or on the Internet who will publish your book within hours, almost free. Once that's done, your book will be available for purchase almost immediately.

Where could people buy your book? From those publishers, from you, or from Web site or brick-and-mortar bookstores—where they probably buy books now. The others make the sales and pay you directly. All you do is spend the income.

Your friends, family, and anybody else can be reading your words within days or weeks from the time you submit the text to what I call "ancillary publishers."

You, in print for sale everywhere! You are just one finished manuscript away! And you needn't learn a thing about publishing, spend a dime creating the pages, squander years getting big-city houses to accept your manuscript, or set up tedious and expensive self-publishing structures.

Nothing like this has ever existed in publishing. I don't want to overdo it, but it really is a sort of miracle.

How to Get Your Book Published Free in Minutes
and Marketed Worldwide in Days

A person who publishes a book appears
willfully in public with his pants down.

Edna St. Vincent Millay, 1892-1950

How to Get Your Book Published Free in Minutes
and Marketed Worldwide in Days

Chapter One

You, a published author?

May I tell you two short stories about folks to whom ancillary publishing may indeed seem miraculous?

A middle school teacher getting unstuck

I met a tall, skinny, bearded lad about 40 who reminded me of a young Ichabod Crane. He told me that he taught seventh grade so he could play.

I was almost afraid to ask him what that meant. He laughed and said that, given his druthers, he'd spend all his time fly fishing.

Turns out that he's locally famous because he has created some weird lures and a unique fishing technique that his colleagues all want to know about. He's also spoken at fishing gatherings—which he loves.

Could he write a book that would be the core of a campaign to get him invited to speak at conventions nationwide and Canada?

"Already got a couple books sort of done," he added, "but nobody seems interested in publishing them—and I sure don't know how!"

Who wants kids' books about warts?

A tiny woman waylaid me as I slipped away restroom-bound during a workshop break. She thrust out her hand and introduced herself. She said most people called her "somebody's grandmother."

7

"I've got 22 kids' books, I illustrated them all, but nobody wants to publish them. I'm making Kinko's rich! What should I do?" (Buying Kinko's stock came to mind.)

I asked if she had any of the books with her. She reached into a satchel and handed me *Louie Has Warts!*

"This is the newest. They all look pretty much alike."

It was first-rate, funny; even the artwork looked professional.

I asked if she was selling many copies, and she said she averaged about 50 a book—but she could sell hundreds just within 20 miles. She could create a new one every month, she said, but she was exhausted with all the folding, stapling, and schlepping.

There must literally be a million Americans with a book in them that will never be seen or read. And how many more thousands of wee books "published" on a copier, or still captive in a digital file, that would change the lives of the writers and thousands of unaware potential readers if they just knew how to get the book quickly and inexpensively in print?

Add to that the professionals who need validation books that show their expertise and articulation. Or ...

* family history and private memoir books that will inform and inspire kin and grand-kin almost forever
* cookbooks with recipes that need trying, sharing, and preservation
* humor books, joke books, funny family or company happenings
* baby books, full of footprints, photos, announcements
* fiction of all kinds and to all ages
* non-fiction, from the full account of Uncle Al's pin and needle shop to the history of soap (or soup)
* a photo-and-text account of the family's trip to Ghana or the Grand Canyon
* a memory book of the twins' high school graduation

* or an odd little book that would have been completely lost but instead monumentally changes the world's thinking

So my book is written to fly fishermen, "somebody's grandmother," and every one of you (and your friends) who know something that the rest of us need to know and who also need a professional-looking vehicle to get it saved and before our eyes.

What follows is an explanation of what you must do to avail yourself of a new means that can convert your words (and artwork, including graphs, charts, cartoons, photos, and much more) into books which will look good, might sell widely, and will remain your property to grow from.

To write what is worth publishing,
to find honest people to publish it,
and to get sensible people to read it,
are the three great difficulties
in being an author.

Charles Caleb Colton, 1780-1832

Chapter Two

Ancillary publishing

Let's start from the beginning...

Do you have a book inside you just shouting to get out? You have something to say and time is running out? If you don't get to it soon, will you just be number one zillion who dies bookless?

Maybe it's a novel, a kid's book, a joke book, or a cookbook? Why not a "how-to" book that shares all you've learned about your job, coaching, or raising teens or rutabagas? Or a 1,000-page revelation of life's real meaning?

Then join the huge club of frustrated would-be book writers who *didn't* write their book in the last 12 months—and probably won't unless they can figure out a way to make all the rest of that, like publishing, happen!

The writing is daunting enough, but with computers, spell check, how-to books, and classes that will fill in the writing gaps, you could probably get the words down and even make them look good.

It's what comes next!

How would you put it together? Where would you get a decent cover? Where can you get it printed—and what part of a king's ransom would that cost?

And even if you could print a dandy little book, how would you sell it? On the street corner? Knocking on doors? How would you get it in bookstores, libraries, Costco, and Amazon.com? How much would be left after paying the middlemen?

That's really the problem, isn't it? It's the whole process, the writing, producing, promoting, shipping, storage ... and the money to do it! The recession isn't helping our confidence much either.

If the big publishers would just call you up and beg! But that's not going to happen. With no books in print, unless

11

you're a celebrity or infamous, you're going to have to make it all happen.

Ancillary publishing to the rescue!

The process is new and it's designed just for you. I call it "ancillary publishing"—I'll explain the terminology a bit later, and the names of the publishers who do it too in a moment.

First, we'll focus on precisely what you must do to get your words and ideas in print just as you want them, professional in appearance, with a full-color, fancy cover, available to buy by anybody interested almost anywhere.

You want a preview of the process before you go any farther? At the risk of scaring you away—each of the nine steps that follow will be explained in detail, and they are easily within any computer user's capacity—here is what you do to get your book published the ancillary way:

1. You write your book.
2. You get it in final, proofed, ready-to-roll format.
3. You slightly transform the final Word/book manuscript into a Word/digital format—and save both.
4. You also write two descriptions of the book.
5. You either create a cover of the bound edition at the publisher's Web site (free) or you have a cover of the book made by your own designer and saved in pdf and .jpg.
6. You save both of the two final Word manuscripts in PDF—you now have four master files.
7. You send your contents and e-book files plus your cover file to LSI to have them send each book version to their respective distribution markets.
8. You use the contents book file to get your book produced and sold in bound form by Lulu, CreateSpace, or Blurb.
9. And you use your digital contents file to get your book into Lulu, Kindle, Smashwords, and Scribd.

In other words, you will write your book, get it in five ready-to-go files (really one text file slightly modified and a cover file), and submit it to as many as seven different book publishers who will have your book ready to go in hours (for the e-book version) and days for the bound, printed copy.

There's no middle-person either. My role is to explain the process on these pages. And you can do the rest of the writing and file prep yourself—or, if you need specific help at any step (it's really easy, and you shouldn't need assistance), you can pay the publishers only for what you need.

I will explain the writing and file prep, then publishing and promotion, in the next three chapters.

Who am I?

A veteran publisher who started creating books in 1981, probably before you were born! I've had 38 books of my own published and have published about 75 more books and products for others. Alas, I've made every mistake you can think of, some repeatedly—and I've had to scale the same hurdles I suggest that you might be facing. But the solutions were much riskier then, much costlier, and far slower before ancillary publishing popped on the scene a couple of years ago.

I first heard about this new process about a year ago, when it was new. But I didn't seriously explore it until five months back, because I simply didn't believe its claims. I've seen a thousand improvements in printing and publishing in 30 years (like cut-and-paste, linotypes, electronic teletypesetting, computers, digital printers, digital attachment submissions, .jpg inserts...), but who would imagine that a publisher would ask you to send them your text and cover so they could pay you to create your book, then sell it nationwide—at no cost to you?

But it's the real thing, and, as I said, it's about as close to a publishing miracle as I've ever seen, particularly for everyday Betty and Bob who have something valuable to share in print.

13

Before ancillary publishing, they had about as much chance of seeing their words competitively published by a professional house as they did of growing more arms! Particularly if they proposed a novel, a kids' book, or anything with colored pages or much artwork.

Most of my 2,000-plus speeches and seminars in the past years were about book publishing and article writing, so I've heard about or seen every obstacle, frustration, and self-inflicted publishing fear imaginable. But now I see a solution at hand for anybody who is literate, has something to say that others want or need to hear, can word process at a basic level, and really wants to be in print.

Incidentally, an additional comment since we probably don't know each other. I have no vested interest in any ancillary publisher. My remarks in their regard, kind or less so, come mostly from my experiences trying to use their software and putting my book(s) on their sites. I am not connected in any way to any of them, other than one employee of one attended a seminar I gave, which was totally coincidental.

How does it work?

While America and the world have plowed through a recession, "ancillary publishing" has appeared with little fanfare.

The system is so straightforward, and frankly so easy to do, that it makes one wary. It almost looks like a con—but it's not. I can see a publishing con blindfolded.

The seven publishing companies involved have taken the best of digital printing, blended it with solid marketing, and put an inspired business plan in action. The companies are reputable and they are unrelated. You share the same vested interests: they make money when your book sells. And it must be good and look good to do that. You get a special bonus: each sale brings you a touch of fame and validation of your skills and expertise.

They will take your final, ready-to-go book text files, add in your cover file, and from those files produce a digital book and/or a bound book. It will be professional-looking, organized and reproduced just as you wrote it, with a fancy colored cover and the title you gave it.

Then most of them will not only sell the book to you, your family, your friends, and anybody else who will buy it, they will also sell it to the key distributors in the U.S. and abroad. One publisher even converts your book into nine different digital reader languages. All you have to do is cash in your part of the sale 60 or 90 days later.

Better yet, the three that produce bound books will show you how to create your book's cover at their Web site in probably less than an hour. (If that's too technical for you, they have a service that will guide you.)

Except for that special help that few will need, all of this costs you nothing—or a token, as I mentioned. (But I will show you two places where you may want to spend a few bucks to reap a lot more income later.)

"Why is this a huge, radical improvement for book authors?"

Long ago there were monks who "printed" books with quills. Later, the printing press appeared in Europe. And authors sold books first, then wrote them if enough people bought.

Move past World War II. If you wanted to be a published author (particularly for novels or children's books), you found a publisher, sent a letter that sold your idea and skills, signed a contract, wrote the book, then waited what seemed like a lifetime to see your words in print—all for about 10% of what the buyer paid, and that begrudgingly sent a couple of times a year by snail mail (although snail mail then usually arrived in a day or two, for 3 cents.)

Then computers appeared and all of the processes got faster and cheaper, the end product got better looking, and all the writers had access to them! Authors could even get their own books printed in volume and shipped in less than a month. Self-publishing emerged and evolved. But self-marketing, outside of the niche fields, didn't, so most of the new one-author enterprises required learning and using new sets of selling skills and tools.

That left the novice book writer with two reasonable choices: (1) the old "big house" query begging to get the prose accepted, with perhaps real begging to stay alive until the royalties arrived, or (2) having to learn and use new skills or means to convert a self-written offering into a self-published life-sustaining product. Their self-publishing profits might be 25%, even 40% if the book was niched, but only after the book-producing and -marketing debts were paid.

Creating profitable books has always followed the 3-P process: preparation, production, and promotion (plus patience and prayer). If you had a book you wanted to write, you simply had to put the words together (or pay a "real writer" to quietly do it for you). But now, with the writing and editing done, when it's ready to foist on a reading public, you have a choice of many no-charge publishers who will do the production and the promotion (or at least the marketing) for you.

Are the ancillary publishers doing this because it's the 21st century and you're a lovely lass or lad? Maybe, but mostly because they, too, have a bottom line. In exchange for you bringing them genius in a file, that is, a book in final form, they will convert your words into a professional-looking book and sell it for part of the money earned. (They may also hope that you're a braggart who also has a huge, book-buying family.)

How much will these modern-day saints pay you? Something between 22 and 85% of the cover price—but most pay in the 35-45% range. For that, after you have entered the enchanted text and cover files into the publishers' software and later proofread the final book, you need do nothing but spend your earnings.

16

Do you see why this excites me? And if you really dreamt of seeing your book in print in your own lifetime, why this new business model throbs with so much potential?

Ancillary Publishing

This group of publishers, and the process they offer, has an awful title that incorrectly suggests vanity press. They are the "minimum service subsidy press."

Let's call them "ancillary publishers," since in fact they offer a two-pronged path that either gives newcomers a back-door way to publish without becoming a publisher or established publishers a secondary way to widely sell books beyond their own conventional publishing efforts.

Thus, ancillary for auxiliary, subsidiary, supplementary, or secondary. All are honorable.

(I know, the term "ancillary publishing" has been around a long time, but it never described an industry, rather a service or a title of an editor who sold a primary manuscript or product, in whole or part, to spin-off buyers, like translations, related articles, booklets, and more.)

There is an unknown part of this miracle, however. Does it have the earning power to keep you and the rest using its means out of the breadlines? We can see the high quality of their production, but it's still too early to see if ancillary marketing can keep enough income flowing for the publishers and us.

That may not be a monumental concern for the one-book newbies mentioned. One book in print may well be enough. The doors only need stay open long enough to sell to the family, friends, and the one potential boss who matters.

It's a three-path process

There are three key things that you must know about ancillary publishing to fully participate.

17

One is how to write your book—really, how to prepare its files for quick acceptance. I'll explain that in Chapter 3.

Two, how to submit those files to the respective ancillary publishers—and perhaps, at the same time, to LSI (Lightning Source) to get POD (print-on-demand) copies for your own use. In Chapter 4 I will talk about what each firm does, how they differ from each other, and an order of submission that makes the most sense. That chapter shows, step-by-step, how to get your book up and produced by each company.

And three, if you help in the marketing, you will sell a lot more books. That's what Chapter 5 says.

Still, it only seems right to add a final chapter for my colleagues, the established publishers, that answers **"How Can Established Publishers Best Use Ancillary Publishing?"**

That chapter, the sixth, clearly isn't for the newcomer. Yet if the starters have success with their books and want to increase their publishing income and expand their empires, it will explain how that can happen faster once they have created an ancillary publishing base.

What do you do first?

The basic question that all publishers must answer first is what your end product will look like, what you need on its pages, and why you are even bothering to do that at all? I mean, really, why bother to even write and publish a book?

So first, if you are going to have the ancillary publishers actually produce your book, you both must get on the same wave length—or money line!

What kinds of books do the ancillary publishers produce? They don't seem to care much about the topic. It could be non-fiction or fiction; for kids, the general population, or seniors; it could have a niche core (like a book for oculists, o-zone specialists, or off-track gamblers); it could be a cookbook, photo collection, memoir; poetry, or the antidote for a heart-broken soul needing a new romance. Or a family tree—that is really up to you.

But ancillary publishers don't publish just anything. You might check before you submit the rankest sex, endless and pointless diatribes, or opuses in yet-to-be-discovered languages.

And there are guidelines. When you submit the book's ready-to-go text file, it must be just that, in the specific software language the publisher uses—probably Word converted to PDF. (I tell you all this in Chapter 4.)

There are some size restrictions, too. Most books will be 5½" x 8½" or 6" x 9", but some can even be square. The length of the book, within reason, doesn't seem important, except that the longer it is, the more your profit is eaten up by the paper costs.

Some of the ancillary publishers print bound books. Most of those have front and back covers, with a spine. The non-fiction bound books usually have a table of contents, chapter headings, a page header or footer, and a closing index.

Other ancillary publishers produce only e-books, to ultimately be digitally downloaded to a computer, phone, iPod, or reading device. In most cases the e-books are about 99% unchanged in content from the final text file of the bound book. But the farther the publishers stray from a basic PDF conversion—that is, they use their own software language—the more things like artwork, images, graphs, charts, and page numbers have to be altered. I'll give details later, but in terms of writing your book that should have little impact at the outset.

Some ancillary publishers produce both bound and e-books.

Don't worry right now what the final product will look like or if it will be on paper or sent electronically. Think now about writing a dandy book that will be bought by scores or millions of readers.

How to Get Your Book Published Free in Minutes
and Marketed Worldwide in Days

There ain't nothing that breaks up homes, country, and nations like somebody publishing their memoirs.

Will Rogers, 1879-1935

Chapter Three

Writing the magic files

The publishing clock starts the moment you submit your book's file(s) to the respective ancillary publisher(s) or printer(s). To put that book in ready-to-print format is the purpose of this chapter.

To publishing veterans the first sections of this chapter are familiar ground, so for them they may be a quick checklist, although the file prep section at the end is a somewhat different way of doing an old thing—and the file chart at the end surely will be helpful later.

Newcomers might find the 22 sections (or steps) far more useful. The goal, in either case, is to help you both create a solid book worth writing and an error-free, attractive manuscript worth publishing.

Let's get writing!

We can talk about writing until the aliens land, but real book writers actually write. So what follows is my system for writing books.

Trust me to know what the end result of book writing must look like for it to get profitably printed. And let's make ancillary publishers proud to have your words going through their presses or servers!

Here are 22 steps, from a shaky idea to the five magic files that you need to follow to enter those gilded ancillary publishing gates.

In publishing it's said that writing the book is easy; all the rest is hard.

Well, in your case, with ancillary publishers eager to put your book quickly into salable shape, then sell it, you have found a way to let experts carry the heaviest load—free. Let's get writing before they catch on!

In one sentence, what is your book about?

This is the most important step you will take; otherwise you will likely spend a year writing or dabbling at five unfinished books—and none will see print!

Fortunately, there's an almost fail-safe way to get your book timely afoot.

First, you write a purpose statement about your proposed book. That is, in one sentence explain the purpose of your book. Let's say the purpose of your book is to show readers how to swim safely from Alcatraz to San Francisco.

Next, convert that one-sentence statement into a working question. The question here is, "How can one swim safely from Alcatraz to San Francisco?"

Then your book is the answer to that working question, plus anything that defines the elements of the question. Here, that would start by defining Alcatraz, swimming, San Francisco, and the facts of the swim.

Type out the working question and tape it to your monitor. Yes, another item hanging from your monitor! It's the judge. It will help you throw out lots of irrelevant facts and war stories that may be interesting in somebody else's book, or another book of yours later, but not here.

Your book is your response to this working question. That response is the reason for your book's existence. Also, if you rigidly adhere to this formula, you will probably write your book twice as fast.

There's one more critical step: make a list of every secondary question that comes to mind from your working question. Questions that must be answered to achieve your purpose. The most obvious of these secondary questions begin with "who, what, why, where, when, or how."

Like who makes this swim? Maybe kids and perhaps a few old people, but mostly those in their 20s-40s—and only those with the physical ability to swim! Answer those six starter questions, the "who, what, why's...," add some more secondary questions, and you have the core of your book outline.

Give the book an order that makes sense—like developmental, chronological, a case study, or whatever. Then sort the secondary questions into that format and, *voilá*, you have a tentative book outline. Those then become the book's chapters.

For example, we might focus on the massive, annual Alcatraz to San Francisco swim and build from there. Our book might be a how-to case study with the reader the key participant. Since the purpose would be to take part in that event, you might start your book's process a year in advance and tell what, step-by-step, the readers must do to progress from near zero (can they swim yet?) to completing the actual feat.

From that, you might add additional chapters about (1) how the actual swim can be done at any time and how that would be arranged, (2) other organized swims from Alcatraz to San Francisco during the year, (3) historical swims (and failures) in the past, (4) the dangers of trying and failing, and so on...

List 3-5 benefits or needs that your book will bring its reader

Why would anybody actually pay for your book, or even read it free, if it doesn't bring the buyer/reader some benefit or meet his/her need(s)? Granted, some folks have to at least look at what you publish, like mates, maybe your kids and folks, and anybody else who will fan you in the midday sun.

The rest, the public, just don't care that much that you wrote a book. Some 200,000 other books were written in the last year. How concerned are you about those books and authors—and you're a book author!

The way you get others to care is to solve their problems or bring them benefits.

How to Get Your Book Published Free in Minutes
and Marketed Worldwide in Days

How do you make others care about your book? Write a legitimate book telling them how to convert soup spoons into solid gold. Get it in print and let readers know of its existence. Not only will they care, they will start hoarding soup spoons!

You can have thousands of readers, maybe millions, thanking you for making their lives better, happier, funnier, more rewarding, easier—but you must write the book that does that first. What can you write about? Almost anything that others will benefit from reading, like a fact-filled, benefit-laden book about effortless exercise or how to write treasure hunt clues, repair their ceiling fan, sell their Studebaker, find a "keeper" mate, or overcome loneliness.

Thus, part of your purpose statement is to identify them and define the benefits that you will bring to the reader or the needs you will help them satisfy.

Is this important? Just if you want to separate potential readers from their closely guarded money and their even more jealously defended reading time! That is, if you want to sell some of the books you write.

Find at least five other books identical or very similar to your book

Yes, you're going to have to read these books, probably twice each—but don't panic. You will be writing your own book at the same time. This isn't a free pass to stop writing while you curl up at the town library!

I know, you don't need to read nobody else's stinkin' books. Your book is unique, singular, unmatched, so... Please, just humor me. If you're smart enough to write a book, you're smart enough not to reinvent the wheel.

You're going to read those books that are like your book because you're going to steal anything of convertible worth from them. They are your opposition, your worth weigher, the standard that others will hold you to. You aren't going to simply mimic and replicate them, but to the degree that your book is different, when you differ from them, it will be by choice and not from ignorance.

Put the book most like yours on top and start reading it.

The first time through you are going to see what working question that book answers. It will almost always be stated in the introduction or first chapter. Then you're going to clarify how the table of contents creates that fulfillment path. Write down every illustration or reference; why is it there? What does it support? See how long the chapters and sections are. Study the foreword, contents page(s), blank page insertions, index, glossary, product page, and biography. How many quotes from others are included, how many anecdotes? Are there footnotes? How are successive referrals addressed (Dr. Tom Jones, Dr. Jones, Jones, Tom, etc.)?

On the second pass you will read the book, start to finish, to feel the style of writing, the flow, the amount and kind of humor, the paragraph lengths—anything that will enrich your sense of how this kind of book is skillfully composed.

What are you doing with all this borrowed wisdom? You're writing down anything that will work for you on a tablet of paper, or in a computer file, probably divided into categories. You'll scan or copy long passages or layouts or a cover or table of contents design and insert or tape them to the tablet. This will be a repository of what you need in your current book (or even a coming book).

By the time you have read five (or three or eight) books like yours, you will know what you have to do to write a book that will bring you, and those near you, proper pride and sufficient content—and will attract eager buyers for every book you write later.

Should we give your book a title?

You bet. Why not start with five—or 15?

You already know the purpose of your book and who will want to read (and buy) it. You have a provisional table of con-

How to Get Your Book Published Free in Minutes
and Marketed Worldwide in Days

tents. So let your mind wander. Take a page or two in your tablet —(or create a clean computer file) and write TITLES on the top. Then make a list. Add and add ... and as new titles come to mind in the coming days, add them, too. (But don't erase: you'll need that erased word later. Just add the modified version below it. You can never have too many.)

Let them marinate. Just don't title too broadly—"How to Dream"— or too narrowly—"Putting Tips for Fat, Twitchy Octogenarian Bad Golfers."

Include the benefits or needs in the title, if you can.

Don't forget your targeted market. If your book is about designing ideal dental offices, don't call it "Ideal Offices." Anybody with an office will think it's for everybody else! But "Dentists: You Deserve a Perfect Office Like These." They will think, "Here's a book with a choice of great offices that I have to look at." Bingo.

Put the list in some provisional order and focus on both #1 and the first five. You will make the final choice much later on. Just keep adding any new ideas as you go along; then forget about a title for now. (You can call it "My Book" in the meantime.)

A personal thought: While I am writing a book, I often rewrite the contents into magazine or newsletter articles. As often, my title also comes from a slight rewording of one of those article titles.

Time to write the back cover of your own book

This is Dan Poynter's idea from *The Self-Publishing Manual*, and I've been slavishly following it for years. It makes huge sense, as odd as it sounds.

For an acceptable, selling back cover you need a subject category, headline, a title (pick your first choice for now), maybe a sub-title, about five or six short selling paragraphs, space for a testimonial or two, a box for the needed data (ISBN number or equivalent, price, format [like trade paperback] and

How to Get Your Book Published Free in Minutes
and Marketed Worldwide in Days

number of pages) or a bar code (the ancillary publisher will provide this), a short bio slug, and a one-sentence selling byte.

Find a paperback nonfiction book in your stacks and look at the back cover to see examples of each.

Let me define the terms.

The subject category is a one- or few-word line in the top left-hand corner that tells where the library and bookstore should display your book. It might be "Reference/Book Publishing" or "Baseball."

Sometimes broad titles need a tighter sub-title. We just published a book that was a devil to title until we found a subtitle that included the fact that the book was about school law. The main title was *Finding Middle Ground in K-12 Education*—but what does that mean? Only when we added, in smaller type as the second deck, *Balancing Best Practices and the Law*, did it collectively make sense and start flying out of our warehouse.

The other terms are obvious. Don't worry about testimonials now—who worth quoting would give you one for a book not yet written? When the book is nearly done, send a digital copy of several proofed chapters to people whose word is respected, and they will very likely give you a testimonial a short sentence or two long.

If you use a bio slug, it will talk about your expertise, qualifications, and recent books. You don't need a photo, although first authors almost always include one! Instead of a bio the first time out (when you might not have much to include that would compel a reader to buy), you might insert a small copy of the front cover art.

Let's look at an actual example, in fact the book just mentioned. Our one-sentence selling byte was "The Middle Ground is the highest ground between leadership and school law." Probably more people will respond to that byte than anything else on the back (other than title[s]), so it must provoke the reader to at least say, "Oh yeah!" Maybe even rush to the computer to order!

27

Let's look at the actual back cover of the *Finding Middle Ground...* book on the next page. I gave the basic copy to the cover designer who then inserted the sparse artwork and colors, plus the barcode once I had the ISBN info and determined the price. Originally, I just inserted blank lines where you now see the testimonials. (We sent early digital copies of the final book text requesting testimonials from leaders in the field. These three were the best.)

Next, I wrote a 500-word explanation of what the book was about. Most of that came from Chapters #1 and #2, which had guided the authors' writing of the text. I imagined I was a school leader or a school lawyer and I told them what we had between the covers that would make their jobs or responsibilities easier to perform and better done. Then I edited it to about 300 words—the size that fit comfortably.

The selling byte in the lower left corner occurred to me early on and I had jotted it down on my tablet. So I later plucked it and planted it where it would do the most good!

Study this example and five other back covers of books similar to yours. Pencil-create one for your book. Put your tongue in your cheek and make promises. Then keep every one of them when you write the book. (Or remove those you can't keep, but replace them with others you can.)

You'll notice that the example uses the title(s) as the headline and puts the testimonials above it. And it limits the bios of the authors to the title of one book only that each wrote—and no photos. But it's full of benefits, it shouts "expertise," and it says that other, respected leaders confirm its "must-read" status.

So nothing is inviolate. The important thing is that potential buyers/readers will either open the book because of what they saw or read on the back or they will straight-line to the order form.

28

Finding Middle Ground in K-12 Education...

"... should be required reading for all ed leadership law classes—practical and relevant."
Jason Leahy, Executive Director, Illinois Principals Association

"... a welcome addition to the professional libraries of administrators, teachers, and parents."
Charles J. Russo, J.D., Ed.D., Panzer Chair in Education and
Adjunct Professor of Law at the University of Dayton

"... a must for school administrators' desks."
Dr. Michael Johnson, Education Director, Illinois Association of School Boards

FINDING MIDDLE GROUND IN K-12 EDUCATION

Balancing Best Practices and the Law

Jim Burgett • Brian D. Schwartz

authors of *Teachers Change Lives 24/7* and *The Law of Homeschooling*

The meanest and sweetest word in education today may be "lawsuit"! It both stops progress cold, and it keeps educators socially guided. Yet two new words are emerging as far more powerful: MIDDLE GROUND, that hallowed dale of compromise between what is required and what works, where problems and issues are first prevented, and if not, resolved.

Knowing the rules is only half the answer. The art of clear and effective leadership is also required when conflict exists between good instructional practices and the law.

Which is where Jim Burgett and Brian Schwartz and their 18 case studies shine. They have a shared goal, to keep readers and leaders out of court and to provide students with a first-class education. Brian masterfully makes complex laws understandable while Jim magically converts discord into solvable win-win situations. On these pages, the two prize-winning educators balance best practices and the law into a compelling book that's full of practicality, reality, humor, and how-to common sense.

Don't be deceived by the fact that it's easy to read and lots of fun. It might just change the legal-administrative school climate nationwide.

The Middle Ground is the highest ground between leadership and school law.

ISBN 978-0-979629-56-3

$24.95

52495 >

9 780979 629563

How to Get Your Book Published Free in Minutes
and Marketed Worldwide in Days

My question when I was new to book writing was why I had to do this at all and particularly why so early when I still didn't know what would actually be on my book's final pages.

The reason is that a back cover outlined early gets your head straight and your purpose well aligned with your selling campaign. It tells, up front, what your book is about, why others will be delighted to read your words, and why they will eagerly part with their funds to have their own copy. It also tells you which promises you must make to attract happy buyers—and what promises you must then make true!

Trust me. Faith.

What should your book look like inside?

That's easy: your book was hiding inside the five or so prep books you read, plus any other books in your category in the library, bookstore, or in your house. You just have to find and fine-tune it.

That is, they are in-print examples of the style you want for your pages. You can copy any other layout or format that you want!

What are you looking for? Probably your book's size, its binding, the cover (paper quality, finish, colors, and layout), and the way the contents inside the covers are designed, like paper color and density, type size and color, whiting (leading) between text lines, margins, use of header and/or footer, what you do with the empty even pages, and more, plus the artwork (images, charts, graphs, photos, and more).

Three guidelines:

1. Look at Dan Poynter's *Self-Publishing Manual* for additional thoughts if you are unsure. (It's a book you should have on your shelf anyway when you consider any form of self-publishing, including ancillary publishing.)

How to Get Your Book Published Free in Minutes
and Marketed Worldwide in Days

2. Find a style you like in one or many of the books you have read, make a photo copy of each item, and simply replicate or modify it on your pages.
3. Some of this won't matter at all because the ancillary publishers will make the lesser decisions for you once you determine the size book (among their choices) that you want.

Let me zero in on some style decisions you must make—then you can mull over the rest until you've finished writing your book and know its final contents.

Book size: The publishers will give you choices, but unless there's another reason, consider a book 5" x 8" or 6" x 9".

Binding: Unless the ancillary publisher has a fancy choice for a specialty book you have in mind, your book will be a bound paperback with a perfect bind, it will be digital, or it will be both.

Cover: We'll discuss this later, but you are either going to design it yourself at Lulu, CreateSpace, or Blurb or you will pay somebody else to do it for you.

Paper color and density: Again, the ancillary publisher will decide, but count on white or off white with black type.

Type: Use a serif type (like Times Roman, Verdana, Tahoma, or Century), probably 11, 11.5, or 12 point for your text; rarely use any type under 9-point; use the same font throughout, and once you have a style and size for the chapter heads and sub-heads, stick with it.

Leading: Don't worry about it since the fonts have the leading built in.

Margins: Think of starting at 1" on all sides. If you like another layout better, use your ruler, move the Word margins, and see if that works.

Header or footer: You'll probably use one or the other, but not both. Centering them removes hassles. No headers on chapter opening pages or before the introduction. You may have

How to Get Your Book Published Free in Minutes
and Marketed Worldwide in Days

to delete the header or footer page numbers in your digital final draft.

Empty pages: In novels, the first chapter starts on the right. There are no empty pages after that. Non-fiction often has every chapter starting on the right, which leaves empty pages on the left. You can leave them blank; most insert quotations or artwork.

Other concerns:

* Don't <u>underline</u>.
* Single space between sentences.
* Don't indent the first paragraph in your chapters but do indent the regular text about three spaces from the left.
* Rarely use **bold** copy in the text itself.
* Don't use **BOLD CAPS.**
* Also, only use CAPS when absolutely necessary.
* *Lots of italic font is hard to read.*
* Don't use "by" on your cover or title page (no "by Lee Lumpkin, just Lee Lumpkin).
* Use no spaces before or after "em" dashes.
* Never use two hyphens -- for an—em dash.
* Justify the text on both sides.
* Activate the hyphenation.
* Steal somebody else's table of contents and index formats.

If you're preparing your book in Word, go to File/Page Setup, and in "Paper" insert 6" and 9" (or the size your book will be) for the whole document. Then return to the "Margins" page and insert 1" on the four sides for the whole document.

Do all of these things and write your first draft in this format. Add any artwork, then print out a copy of several chapters and see how it looks. That's when you start moving things around or modifying the appearance. Just don't worry about it until you are nearly done—or you'll spend so much time fidgeting that you'll either forget what your book is about or you will lose interest!

32

What must your book contain?

Take an hour, go some place where you won't be interrupted, write down your purpose statement again, and then write down everything you want in your book. Don't worry about the order, where you'll find the information, or anything else. Just write, list, envision what others would want, ask questions, draw arrows if related ideas pop out from earlier ideas, even make boxes or pages for follow-up books or related topics.

When that's done, review those earlier books you read. What more should you add? Now's the time to zero in on the heart of your book.

If you think of more later, of course you can add that in, too.

Put all of this on the same tablet of paper lest your genius be left in 10 different places. This will save you hours of hunting later.

It's time to give it order, an angle, and a table of contents

Time to sort all of that information into logical sections called chapters!

You can do it on paper, of course, or if most of your contents are a huge pile of notes, examples from others' books, doodles, and photos, you can put them into logical piles—or you can do a bit of both.

Let's say your book is a running diary of family events and happenings. Your table of contents might be eight sections with such thrilling names as: pre-1800s, 1800-75, 1876-1900, 1901-1915, l916-1939, 1940-1945, 1946-1990, 1991-present. Whew, that *is* exciting!

You get the idea. If it's a book on gardening, it might be divided into the seasons. Or if it's how to fix a clock, the steps you must follow to get the thing ticking.

33

The purpose of chapters is to help the reader see where the book goes and how they can return to a certain section—or even, heavens forefend—read ahead! Nor do you need clever titles at the outset, or ever. But they have to make sense in a logical way. They are also great to use to give those piles of contents some meaning.

Incidentally, your novel doesn't need headings for chapters—but it sure needs chapters or you might as well just start with the finale and save paper! Rather than a table of contents for fiction, you'll at least need a detailed outline or you will kill off Cousin Charley before he's even born!

One more thing—and it's important, too. You must determine the position that you as the author of this book will take in relation to the material and the reader. In other words, what is the angle your book takes toward its subject? Are you an expert sharing expertise? An information gatherer and explainer, a sort of distant storyteller without responsibility for what is said? Is the material to be shared objectively or subjectively? Why is this important? Because once mounted, you can't change horses. Best to pick the horse now and have a fun ride.

Will this book be done in your lifetime?

Yes, if you set up a schedule and stick to it.

The truth is the world has somehow thus far survived without your book. It will also continue to plod forward if you fink out, though the poorer for it. So it probably doesn't much care about your excuses.

Novelists often write two to five pages a day, unedited. Old veterans can plunk out 10-20. Somebody wrote the story of the seven-day war in five days. Seasoned writers work rain or shine, indoors. Some rest from writing on the Sabbath; some also rest when the Bears play or the Ladies Math Society meets.

My observation? The more days you don't put in at least an hour or two on your book, the less likely it is to see literary light.

So here's another task. Create a pace you will maintain, set completion goals, and reward yourself—probably with fine food or a couple of days of fun—when you hit key milestones.

And if you fall behind, don't quit. A measuring tool for many writers is this: however long it takes you to write the first draft, double it and that will be how long it will take you to send the five magic files to the eager ancillary publishers.

You need a calendar, conviction, and marked goal dates.

It's also time to give your book carrying weight

You need to have your book in three places: in your computer (seeable on the monitor), on a USB flash drive just in case, and in a three-ring binder.

The first is obvious. The second gives you peace of mind and lets you work on others' computers and keep your results safe and transferable. You simply save that day's work on both the hard drive and the flash drive at the end of each session. (I even pay Mozy to download and save it elsewhere, too. Over-kill?)

The third may seem redundant yet it allows you to work on your book whenever you are unlinked, like in the doctor's waiting room or in a park enjoying the summer sun without having to trudge a laptop.

Most of your "extra" work so far is being saved on a tablet. Now it's time to divide that into its most comfortable parts and give it a protective three-ring cover. Buy some dividers for the chapters, print your copy on three-ring paper as it is created, insert the tablet segments where they belong, and also tape in all of the remaining loose notes and clippings where they best fit, so you can keep all the primary and supporting data at hand in one place.

If you insert a few blank pages in each chapter as well, it's surprising how often you will use them to leave critical notes and thoughts, which you can use when you reach those pages to write the text or to edit it later. The trick is to keep this folder with you pretty much all the time.

How do you write a first draft?

As quickly as possible—and do it first!

Let me share an inside secret on how you can separate the newbies from the veterans. The latter race through the first draft while the first timers belabor every word, parse thrice every phrase, and start again and again and again.

The vets know that their initial inspirations and starter lines will surely be edited and that half of what they write down will never see light—nor should it—as first captured and saved. In fact, they will do that editing themselves later when they bring their prose up to par, and beyond.

But it's new ground for the uninitiated. They seem to be offended that gilded words don't fall each time they are commanded and that anybody, even themselves, would dare to change what they have created. Or chiseled. So they write and rewrite and delete and write again, and it's any wonder that a page a day ever gets completed—however well crafted (and later inappropriate) it is.

So let me tell you once. (Yes, I'm a vet with 1700+ freelance articles and those 38 books in print, and, yes, it took me a few years to catch on.) You look at your purpose statement (taped to your monitor), you read the chapter title, you look through your notes (now in your binder), and you just start writing. It's easier if you sub-divided the chapter into logical points or those secondary questions. But you don't worry much about what you put down. You can always move the words and thoughts around later. And if you draw a blank? Just type a bracketed box that says: fill me in with facts.

How to Get Your Book Published Free in Minutes
and Marketed Worldwide in Days

A perfect example. This morning I was responding to an e-mail and for the life of me I couldn't think of the word "template." So I wrote "... if you create a [ ] you needn't continually reformat..." I put the reply in the draft file and went on with other tasks. Out of nowhere, about 20 minutes later, popped "template"! So I found the draft, replaced the brackets, and sent off the message. A banal example but I don't want a memory lapse to slow down a sentence or thought in flow.

Don't edit as you write. Don't worry about spelling. Don't even worry much if you hit a dry well and have lots of empty brackets [ ] awaiting later inspiration. Your goal is to finish that chapter or section at that sitting.

You do your research off hours or after the first, rough draft is finished. And don't spend forever writing. I'm good from sun-up (or earlier if it's a restless night) for two or three hours, rarely until lunch (at 11). And that's it. Tomorrow I'll pick up where I left off. The rest of the day is for the rest of my life. And, yes, sometimes I trot off to the library to read up on something I left undone that morning or to see what the sun comes up over in Inhambupe, Brazil, because I need that for my book to make sense, but not very often. After all, it's just a first draft and I may replace Inhambupe with Ouro Preto or Rio...

It's time to get your book going and done, to create a base to be tightly edited later, added to, expanded, and filled with the details that make it fun to read and valuable to own. This is the *durance vial*, the tough stuff, the bedrock that you build from to create a book that you will be beaming about and the ancillary publishers will be chomping to produce. Usually two or three months of no-nonsense writing.

A final thing. What you write stays in your head, your file, your flash drive, and your binder. It's raw stuff, the spelling probably off, verbs that don't match the nouns—so what? It's how winners write the first drafts of their books. And if you don't run like a winner, you probably won't finish the race.

Which means that if you show the rough stuff to others (like secretaries, mates, or anybody who will look at it), they

37

will see that the text is lousy and they won't believe that you're a writer. Worse, they will correct the errors and tell you how it should sound and what you should say and how it should be said.

To prevent that, you have two choices. You can finish every day with polished prose, lots of it unusable later and created at the cost of hours of useless editing, or you can just keep your words to yourself, with a promise to those who want you to succeed that they will get to see it the minute the final, polished draft is ready to print. If that doesn't satisfy them, tell them Gordon Burgett said that he would report you to the prose police if you showed raw copy before its time.

Let's talk about research

Sometimes books don't need much research at all. If your book is about a little girl spending a day at the circus with her grandparents, a quick refresher on what one sees or does at a circus is probably enough.

Or you might be writing about some "how-to" process where you are already well informed, current, and understand what the reader doesn't know but should.

But most other books need more, accurate information to merit their existence. Even novels have to ring with authenticity. For example, it's best to use a poison that's lethal if that's the murderer's intent. Or the characters must speak in the jargon used at the time of the book's setting about things known then. Don't have Cicero eating quiche or Florence Nightingale jogging while she listens to an iPod.

Which means that somewhere during the writing process, mostly before, you have to gather up the facts and anecdotes you need, and maybe test the theories or machinery that your pages will propose. Quotes add authenticity to books, too, actual quotes, historical ones, or factional imaginings (which is fiction but as close to fact as possible, like what you think Queen Isabella actually said, in a biography).

38

The accuracy and relevance of your research directly affects your expertise. If you want the reader to believe you, truth is the cornerstone.

And if you say you did something, what you write had better add credence to that claim. Use the correct terms. If you are writing from authority to dentists, don't refer to cavities or caps or they will know you're an outsider.

Rather than try to guess how you might do better research (or do it faster), may I suggest some thoughts that work for me? They address two components: (1) the uniqueness of and the need for your book, and (2) where you might go to find new information.

The uniqueness of and the need for your book

These are some questions you might ask about fine-tuning your book to strengthen its distinctiveness and increase its buying demand:

* In addition to the five or so books you already read about your topic, what else has already been in print about it in, say, the past decade? Are those books still applicable or have changes in the field (or society) made them obsolete? Were they widely sold? How much did they cost? How long were they? Do they contain illustrations? How many? What kind? Do they have bibliographies?

* What is about to be published about your topic? (Check *Forthcoming Books in Print* in the library.) Can you get a copy of this new book now? (Books are often available months before their "publication date.") The cost and length of each?

* Since you now know about the other books that are or will be available to your potential readers, how could you slant or direct your book's focus to make it truly different, better, and a more wanted book? Or is that necessary?

39

* How can you increase the perceived value of your book? Include a foreword by a well-known expert in the field? Write with a co-author with wider recognition? Create how-to guides, checklists, or a companion workbook? Should you get testimonials for the cover or sales flyer?

* Could you slant your book so it will create interest in your giving related seminars, workshops, speeches, or classes? Could it be restructured to be more sought by associations that the readers belong to?

* If illustrations are needed for your pages, are any of those that are used in the other books desirable and accessible? Their cost? Will the rights holder permit their use? Or can the illustrations be developed or purchased elsewhere or in another way? Where? How? Again, the cost?

Where you might go to find new information

Here are some solid starter thoughts:

* Start with a keyword list. Think, if you need the four (or six or ten) words that best describe your topic, what would they be? Create two columns on a piece of paper. Put those keywords in the first column.

* Head to Google (or more specific search engines) and type in the keywords, one at a time. See how often those interested in your topic seek information about it using those terms. Then write down in the second column all of the closely-related words or word combinations that appear next to or with your keyword.

How to Get Your Book Published Free in Minutes
and Marketed Worldwide in Days

* Also check www.spacky.com to see how often these keywords are used on three key search engines, plus what other keywords it suggests.

* Study the links that the search reveals, plus the organizations and other sources providing related information. Follow up on the most relevant links.

* Don't forget the library. First check the magazines and newspapers most related to your topic. Ask the angels of the stacks, the reference librarians, how to do this quickly and thoroughly. Let them help you develop a specific hunt for the kind of information you need to make your book up-to-date and sufficiently comprehensive.

* Ask them if you have computer access through their library to Lexis-Nexis articles and news sources, and, if so, how that can be done from your home. That's a gold mine.

* Have you interviewed anybody for your book, if it's appropriate or needed? There are books about the technique, but it's hardly mysterious. You can interview them in person, by phone, or through email. (If you tape, ask permission. If they say no, write fast!)

Know something about the person you wish to interview before you make the contact, know basically what you want from that interview, prepare your questions in a logical order, and then contact them. (Once I wanted to interview then Governor Adlai Stevenson, so I called his office to see if I could set that up. In short, he answered the phone—and said he had about six free minutes right then if I was ready to go!)

Tell them you are in the middle of writing a book about ___ and you'd like to share their thoughts or knowledge about three specific things. (If it's by phone, tell them it will take less than 15 minutes.) The book will be published in ___, and, of course, you'll send them a copy when it sees light. Get to the point quickly—and let *them* talk.

41

Finally, be accurate in quoting. If you don't understand something, ask them to explain it in a different way. If you don't hear them, ask them to repeat it. Thank them. Get their address so you can send them a book copy.

* Doing research is not a permission slip that allows you to hide at the keyboard or in the stacks rather than write and publish your book. It's an in-and-out card so you can publish lots of books while you're in the pink!

Do you want artwork (illustrations) in your book?

Artwork is a general term that includes the whole range of illustrations, like photos, line drawing, images, graphs, charts, diagrams—those things you add to make the text more interesting, less dull, or more clearly understood. Or add beauty or visual clarification to the pages.

There's an issue with some forms of ancillary publishing and most artwork: unless it's preserved in PDF format, it's usually impossible to sensibly include in the e-book versions. We'll address that near the end of this chapter and in even greater detail in the chapters that follow.

But let's say that none of that is a problem. Then your first issue is finding and getting the artwork you want on your pages.

Since I don't use much artwork in my books, my suggestions here may be too general. Still, I have published others' books with artwork, so here are six starter thoughts.

* Unless it is imperative to creating the kind of book you want, keep the artwork to a minimum because it takes up paper space, it is often hard to place precisely where it works best, it costs money, and it may not work well at the digital level however it is saved.

* Unless your book uses color throughout or in specifically designated all-color sections—which is complex to do, costs a lot, and may put the book's price out of a comfortable buying range—the artwork will be in black and white.

* Unless you create the artwork, you will usually need to purchase it. If it is created for you, use a work-for-hire contract so the rights are always yours.

* Illustrators are often the least reliable of the book-creation contributors when it comes to sending samples to choose from and meeting specific deadlines. It's best to request everything weeks early, then keep the pressure applied until it arrives. You must do your part too: pay them on time and give proper acknowledgement (or credit) in the text.

* How do you find the illustrator(s) you want? No mystery here. Mostly by asking friends or other publishers. You can check the search engines, too. If you see something particularly well done that could be adapted (even in concept) to your pages, ask the publisher who created it, then contact that person for a bid.

* Can you use your mate, kid, or cousin to do your illustrations? If the end result is what your book needs, why not? But they still must meet the deadlines and sign a work-for-hire contract. If you do it yourself, you needn't sign the contract—but it's hard to fire yourself if you dally or your artwork looks amateurish.

What if you want to use others' words or artwork on your pages?

Fine, within reason. It *is* your book.

If it's just text and it's dated (say 100 years plus), use it. It's good to inject a bit of Lincoln or Pedro II! Or if it's from public figures and was said publicly, even yesterday, you can probably use it, too. Particularly if it appeared in a government-issued publication, which is almost never copyright protected.

You can use just plain facts, too. Copyright only protects the words in the order in which they are used. I might say in print "The Mayans at their peak never saw horses. Horses had long since disappeared in the Americas, and their descendants only reappeared when the first Spaniards reached the Yucatan Peninsula." You can use any fact from those two sentences any way you wish, but you can't use the words in that order because how the words are used together is the artistic creation that copyright protects.

Or you can paraphrase. For example, you might say that Gordon Burgett, a pre-historian of the Americas, contends that Mayans never saw or knew of horses before the Spaniards arrived in the Yucatan. You needn't use my name or the reference either.

But if you are going to pluck the actual words out of copyrighted or privately-owned sources, you will probably have to get permission to quote that material. That includes text, images, photos, graphs, charts, software, and other artwork. It excludes titles and interviews you personally conducted, but it definitely includes poetry, music, lyrics, and personal letters.

Mind you, I'm not a literary attorney, so if this is a concern to you, you may want to get legitimate legal advice.

What would a "Permission to Quote" letter look like? See www.gordonburgett.com/permissiontoquoteletter.htm for an example we have used for decades, plus some comments that should be useful.

Time to wrap up the first draft!

Like a new home you've been thinking about and planning for years, the last bricks of your book are almost laid and the roof is just a few days away!

Books seem simple enough from afar: covers, pages, a bit of organization, writing, tidying up, and off to the press. But it's not that simple, is it? Like the house, there always seems to be a new nook to finish, wires, pipes, insulation...

Guess what? You've been pounding out the words like a good soldier. You're almost ready to tidy up!

How do you finish that first draft? You write the last words of the body, go back and readjust the table of contents to match the modified chapter heads, and look one last time at spell check warnings.

This is when I write the Introduction, once I know what I'm introducing. Keep it short, a page or several. Here's where you tell the reader what the book is about, why you wrote it, what question it answers, and who deserves special thanks for their help, both with the book and in your life that led to its creation. Don't forget your mate and family, especially in the first book. Read other introductions to get the customary flavor. Do you need one? Probably.

Open up a book and go to the first page: the title, sub-title, and author. Yep, it's time to pick out the title—you can't wait forever. Nothing is as important as the title so do as we said earlier: make a list and eliminate as you go along.

The page that follows in all books is called the *volta face* page. Just model yours after others'. Include the copyright info now, your address(es), First Printing, the (month and) year, credit to the cover designer and proofreader, your ISBN if you have one, your ancillary publisher if asked to be acknowledged here (you can do that at the last minute in your final file), and perhaps your legal disclaimer. Later, fill in the TX form, needed to register your book and get it copyrighted, after the book is printed and you have two copies to send to the Library of Congress, with the fee.

To see a copy of a *volta face* page, go to the front of this book. It follows the title page.

It includes a copy of a sort of stock legal disclaimer that we modify and use in almost all of our books. Just change the wording and it may work well for you.

If you have a Dedication, it might go next (or after the Table of Contents, which should start on the odd-page (right) side. Don't be painfully gushy or sound too amateurish in the Dedication.

If you include your biography, that can go in front or back. That's a good place to hide your photo, too.

Your index (always a good idea) will be composed last, so just leave space now.

Finally (unless you can think of something unique that your book must have but most others don't), if you have blank pages at the end, you may wish to include summaries of other books or products you also have available for readers to buy. Only include those that will be around for a long time. And why mention a price that will be changed as the copies of your book age? Rather, send those interested in each item to a landing page that will give more details and the current cost and formats (like bound book, e-book, audio CD, and booklet). Then send the buyer to your Web site order form for all purchases (which, in turn, may run them back through the respective landing pages for actual ordering).

Once you have almost all of the parts in place, print your book on your own printer so you can see how it will look when it comes back later from the book's publisher or printer.

Treat yourself to some huge reward. You are almost done!

Except that you now must take those printed pages, go somewhere else where you can focus, take out a red pen, and read from start to finish. Make a big mark at every error, at anything that looks ugly and you want to change, and at anything that you don't want as is in your final book.

As important, whenever something doesn't make sense, could be better said, needs more examples, or is too flabby and needs pruning—anything that isn't ready to go—put a big question mark or circle where corrections are required.

Then make all of the modifications. Don't fret if this takes days rather than minutes—better that or it will take a lifetime to stop kicking yourself for letting un-corrections slip through.

You're still not done. Print it out again, and read it through again. Only when it really is ready to go, do you continue.

What do a select few think of what you've said?

Letting others read your book at this stage is controversial, but probably wise if it's your first book (or even your fifth), until your eyes get toughened up.

Those you ask to read your book must be told that this is the final first draft and that the book has not been professionally proofread. Nor are you asking them to proofread it (unless there are factual or procedural errors), but rather to tell you if it's working at this stage and how it might be improved or clearer.

Let your mate (or gal friend or buddy) read it—finally. Also send it to somebody who knows what you are writing about and can zero in on the technical flaws. For example, another cook will have better literary taste for your cookbook than, probably, your grandfather.

Professionals often let their colleagues read one chapter, for advice and flaw-finding. They might also ask, if the reader finds the book worthy, would they send a short testimonial, right then or after they've read the full book? Sometimes I send three samples of the kinds of testimonials that might be used on my cover or primary selling flyer. Often enough they will say, "I like testimonial #2. Why not just add this (their name and title or book they wrote) to it?"

Note that anybody who reads the final draft gets a free copy later and probably gets recognition in the acknowledgements.

Final thoughts. Busy people are just that, and some (maybe many) will decline your singular offer to read your book. Don't be offended. The day will come when you will do the same.

How to Get Your Book Published Free in Minutes
and Marketed Worldwide in Days

Probably worse are those who agree, then respond with at best tepid praise, often blended with numerous suggestions and quixotic question marks. They are almost as maddening as the kin whose entire response is "wow!" or "you wrote a book!" Or nothing, as they slip the book back on your stoop or desk. The problem is that you don't know if the book really stinks, sort of stinks, or they stink because you proved that you can not only read, you can write!

The second draft is faster...

This is what I consider the final-write draft, with (almost) all of the last changes inserted in the file so it can get its final proof-reading.

I recall reading Dick Perry (in *One Way to Write Your Novel*, one of my favorite writing books) suggesting that you set your manuscript aside for two weeks before you write the final draft, to get some perspective after a long, almost-daily courtship putting it together. Makes sense for fiction or non-fiction.

Mostly, I've done that—to great benefit. What seemed obvious while I was feverishly composing just seemed dimwitted a couple of weeks later. I found myself deleting and restructuring and adding a chapter or combining two. And that was before I looked at others' suggestions!

Perry also recommended boiling out most of the adjectives—how many do you need to get into a pristine forest?—and pruning anything ending with an "ly," along with most of the other adverbs. I took that to heart, too, and it made my prose cleaner and clearer.

Then you check what the others have said about the sections you asked them to read. Your first question, "Will that better serve your book's purpose?" If so, is it an improvement?

Sometimes one suggestion will give you a completely different perspective on how to better explain your context. Or it will indicate steps you left out or erroneously deleted. The comments more often contain wee changes that require a yea or nay and ten minutes of repair.

When the body of the book is as good as you can make it, look again to see if there are any changes in the table of contents. Also look at the final layout to see if, in the bound edition, you are going to have blank pages you want to fill. I use quotations from others related to my theme, so all this tells me now is that I must comb the quote books and get 6-10 solid quotations, plus the birth-death dates of each person quoted. I put those in a file and guard them until the next step.

Is the book ready to be read by a professional proofreader? The only thing left out is the index and the pagination.

Time for professional eyes

What will kill a reader's fervor fastest? Misspellings, punctuation errors, endless paragraphs, no flow, and nonsense.

If somebody asks another, "How was ____ (your) book?" and they respond, "I couldn't get into it. He can't spell." Or they say, "It didn't make any sense...," you probably lost that potential reader forever.

So you need a no-nonsense professional with the eyes and mindset to carefully go through your final second draft and check every word, every phrase, every section, and every chapter of the whole book to make certain that those fatal shortcomings don't sap the worth out of otherwise good ideas, valuable life-changing suggestions, and your ticket to acknowledged expertise.

Where do you find this literary angel? Not in your family or among your friends. They usually have too much vested interest in agreeing with you or at least keeping you happy. You need a person who simply tells you like it is (maybe with compassion).

How do you locate them? Ask other publishers or professional writers. Check Google. Ask local newspapers, businessfolk, or ad agencies who they recommend and why. Look at www.guru.com or www.elance.com; then check their credentials very closely. (Be certain that American English is their native tongue.) Expect to pay from $150 to many hundreds.

Also ask how they work best: do they want to write on printed paper or will they make corrections (in markup; see View in Word) directly on your digital copy? If the latter, do you understand the markup process? (Word's Help section will decipher it, sort of.) And do you want them to make the actual change or suggest it to you, for you to do?

Mind you, you needn't correct or modify your book text as they say. For years I gladly used a woman who was superb with context and commas but was very uncomfortable with humor (despite the fact that she was personally quite humorous). So my paper copy returned with giant question marks next to anything that even suggested mirth—and all the punch lines had another, dour alternative written above! Granted, a few times she saved me from printing something sophomoric, but I refused to throw out the fun just for form. It's always your choice.

It usually takes several weeks to get the proofreading done and the draft adjusted. You must double-check every correction later. Where I've printed errors, about 90% of them were corrections I didn't see or corrected incorrectly. But the reader doesn't know: you look as stupid or inattentive whatever the cause.

A final set of related steps and it's time to get your five magic files ready for the ancillary publishers.

Once all of the corrections are made in your file and the artwork is firmly in place, you must decide if you will use running pagination (chapters simply begin where the previous chapter ends, on the right or left side—fine for fiction) or the chapters start only on the right side (odd pages), which is common for most non-fiction.

If the latter, will you use any artwork or quotations on the empty left-side (even) pages? If so, now is the time to place any text or images in the file.

How to Get Your Book Published Free in Minutes
and Marketed Worldwide in Days

Then you will know your final pagination, and you can insert the correct numbers into the table of contents.

At last, you can finally produce your index, if your book uses an index (fiction doesn't).

Of course, there are professional indexers that are used by the big houses, but that's an expense for a small book that you needn't bear. Take your final printed text copy, circle the key words you would expect to find in an index of your book, add to those words the most important words in the chapter headings, and make a combined list. Open the edit/find box and subject each word in your list to its own hunt, then write down each page number found next to the word in your list.

For example, if yours is a law-related book, you might include the word "lawsuit." Then go to your Edit key, open the "find" box, and type in lawsuit. If you find useful references at, say, pages 12, 56, 59, 98, and 201, then those are the numbers you would put after "lawsuit" in the index. (But beware if you type in "laws" that you don't include the references to lawsuit since what you are seeking is also part of the longer word.)

When you have your list completed, alphabetize it, and tell the computer to put the numbers in order. (You can do this in your sort file, in Word's Table section.) What's left is for you to combine consecutive numbers, so if the list says, 7, 8, 9, 12 you will alter it to read 7-9, 12.

Write INDEX on the top, probably reduce the type size, modify the spacing, put it in two columns, check closely, and you're ready to go!

(Yes, this can also be done through software. If you know how, go to it. My way takes about three hours. And yes, it may not be quite as good as a professional indexer would do it. Your choice. I won't tell.)

Your book needs a cover?

It needs three kinds of covers, but they can all be designed from the same model.

1. Your bound books will require a full cover, meaning a front, a spine, and a back.
2. Sometimes in ancillary publishing your bound book will be too thin to use a spine, so in those cases you will need a cover that is just front and back, without a specific spine.
3. And your e-book will only need a front cover.

In ancillary publishing, there are two ways to get a cover.

In the **first way**, probably free, you design your bound book covers at Lulu, Blurb, and CreateSpace. If you have specific artwork in mind, plus a set text composition for the back, you can probably use it on any or all of these three. But each of these covers will be distinct. They might look alike, but they will only work for what you create on that particular site. And there are limitations on what you can design. (The instructions aren't that easy to follow either.)

These bound book covers will also have specific and different bar codes with ISBN-like numbers on the back that can be used only for that publisher's version.

If you create your covers this way, you will also need to create your own cover for the other e-book versions that the other ancillary publishers will produce and sell for you. You can't use the bound book covers I mentioned, although you can probably closely imitate the best and use the same title, sub-title, and artwork you used before.

My suggestion for your e-book cover, if it isn't part of the whole cover, is that the title and sub-title be fairly large and bold, even at the sacrifice of beauty. That's because e-books aren't bought by their covers. At best, the cover is seen in thumbnail catalogs where all you need is for the title(s) to be pleasantly balanced and clearly readable.

Let me insert a strong bias here. I suggest **a second approach** where covers (and their ISBN number) are concerned. (But if your book is going to be published solely by one ancillary publisher, forget this bias and just create your cover on their software.)

The bias says that any book good enough to be widely published by the ancillary publishers should also be a core product of your own (perhaps new) self-publishing company—and for that you want the very same cover and ISBN number on all bound book copies, yours and the ancillary publishers'.

Alas, that costs money: $27.50 for each ISBN number (available in lots of 10 for $275) and from $150-500 to get a solid, professional cover in the three formats I describe above: a full cover, one without a spine, and an e-book front cover. That cover artwork should be provided in both .jpg and .pdf formats, plus the cover files should be usable for fliers, business cards, and in other promotional ways.

Then you simply submit your own cover with your ISBN in your bar code to each of the ancillary publishers to use in their production and sale. That's precisely what I did with my test book (more details in the next chapter) and it worked fine with every publishing house. And I could then release the same book simultaneously for my own in-house and commercial sales. The most important thing, all of the books looked the same and all were tied together with my ISBN.

Comments made earlier in this chapter about artwork and illustrations also directly apply to finding a cover designer and setting up the delivery schedule and work-for-hire contract. Unless you are gifted in book cover design (which means that others would pay you to design for them), I suggest that you either use the templates at Lulu, CreateSpace, or Blurb or hire a cover done by a professional.

It's said that people buy books by the cover. That may be a bit less so with the Web, but it's still a huge factor in their choice. So don't make your cover look like you did it with a ball point pen in 40 minutes.

A friend once told my seminar of book publishers that if they would have their gravestone chiseled with a sledgehammer

53

and a nut picker, then they should design their own book covers!

Your task here, then, is to hire a book cover designer and set a date certain (tell the designer the delivery date is at least two weeks earlier) or to create a simple e-book front cover (that you might do, with care, on your own) and hold off on using the cover templates suggested until it's time to submit the entire book.

Magic file #1 (and its PDF buddy, #2)

Magic files are what this chapter is ultimately about. Do them and your book is all but flying out of a printer ready to shock, amuse, and delight your friends—and make you some well-deserved money.

You've been storing your book in a Word file (probably) and upgrading and editing and polishing up that text until it's now just as you want it to look in print, in the ink-on-paper (bound book) or digital forms.

You've given it the read-through to see that all the chapters, quote inserts, artwork, page numbers (in a header or footer)—everything—are precisely how you want them.

And you've read every word one last time. As far as you can see, it's both errorless and full of needed information. You're excused if you're puffing with well-deserved pride.

That file is Magic File #1, in its native tongue, .doc. You could tell the printer to crank out two or 10 or 200 copies of your book as it is in that file, and they would be legitimate books that you could bind and sell.

Yet you want the book to have that professional touch, and you've chosen the ancillary route to make that happen. One publisher accepts the .doc file, so there you are almost ready to publish. But the other two want your text in PDF so you need another, quick step to make that happen. You must convert the book into PDF, and when that's done you will have Magic File #2.

Let's quickly define PDF to help you complete the second file.

According to *Webopedia*, PDF "stands for *Portable Document Format,* a file format developed by Adobe Systems. PDF captures formatting information from a variety of <u>desktop publishing</u> <u>applications,</u> making it possible to send formatted documents and have them appear on the recipient's <u>monitor</u> or <u>printer</u> as they were intended."

I think of it as taking your text (in .doc) and making a file-long picture of it (in PDF). The task is to make the text and picture look exactly alike (or almost).

You (or somebody) need PDF software to take your .doc file and save it in that universal format. Adobe sells it, but there are many other, less expensive versions, too. We use ScanSoft PDF Professional 4, and we simply tell it to convert the .doc file (here, Magic File #1). It is included in some MAC and Windows programs too, like the new Windows 7.

First, though, put the original Magic File #1 in another folder so it is preserved, unchanged. Make a copy of that original; then tell the PDF software to save your copy of Magic File #1 in a PDF file. The new PDF version will appear on your monitor.

Usually, it will look different than File #1. Most likely the page spacing will have popped, which means that in the conversion some words, lines, or images didn't quite fit, so in this version some of the items will appear on the following page. Since what you see on the monitor is how the text will be printed by your publisher, you have to make some adjustments on your copied File #1 so the two look alike.

Make a note of anything that is different (and wrong) in the PDF version. Then go back to your copy of File #1 and alter it so the errors in appearance disappear the next time you copy it. That usually means that you find the places in the original text where the page popped. Go to Insert/page break and insert the page break symbol where you actually want the page to break. Then save File #1 again, with those changes, and tell the soft-

How to Get Your Book Published Free in Minutes
and Marketed Worldwide in Days

ware once more to convert the copy into a PDF version. Check it again! If it acts up, continue to move copy and insert the break marks (or move the copy forward or around a bit) until the PDF version is precisely how you want your book to look, even though it might be slightly different from the original.

When what you see on the monitor in the PDF file is the same or acceptably similar to Magic File #1, save it as Magic File #2. (We usually run that PDF copy through our printer, take it to a neutral corner [like a park bench or a pizza parlor], and give this #2 file yet one more reading to make doubly sure that it is what we want.)

When you are fully satisfied, then definitively save that final PDF copy as Magic File #2—and move it safely to the folder where you are hiding Magic File #1. Two down!

At this point you have print copy for the three ancillary publishing firms that produce bound book versions: Lulu, CreateSpace, and Blurb.

But you need two more files because you want to sell essentially the same book digitally, as an e-book the ancillary publishing way.

Incidentally, should you later find errors or you want to amend or change the original book, you revert to this 1-2 combination again. You make the changes in #1, you save that in #2, and you look closely at the second, altered PDF version to see that it is what you want to print. I would call those Magic File #1 Book 2.doc and Magic File #2 Book 2.pdf. (Note: we replace "Magic File" with the actual abbreviated book title, like "lobstercookbook#1.doc").

Over time, if changes occur, you may also want to keep a quick log (it can be written on the outside of your paper file folder or saved simply as "book log" in your final copy folder) telling which version went where. So the log might say:

booktitle#1.doc—original, to all ancillary publishers, 1/10/10
booktitle#1Book2.doc—replaced original for all in-house
    books printed after 4/10/10

> booktitle#1Book3.doc—"revised, updated edition," replaced book2 for all in-house books printed after 4/10/12

You'll also want to enter the other four files on the paper file folder or the copy folder as they change.

The e-book magic file #3 (and its buddy, #4)

You can sell your book digitally the moment you complete Magic Files #1 or #2, if you provide it to the buyer as a direct download. (That's right, your book exists the moment these files are proofed and ready to transfer. It needn't be printed in bound form nor must it formally be saved in special e-book format, as we will explain in a moment. Which means that your nose will not grow if you now call yourself a published author. Congratulations!)

Let's refer to those files (#3 and #4) as direct downloads of Files #1 and #2. They should look exactly like the files themselves on the monitor of the person to whom they are downloaded and can be printed out so that the pages look identical to your printed pages.

But you may want to make some modest modifications in File #1 so the e-book digital versions will read better and be more useful in the ancillary publishers' software languages where it will go.

First, though, which ancillary publishers handle e-books? Kindle, Smashwords, LightningSource, Lulu, and Scribd.

To do that you will now create Magic File #3. In fact, probably twice—but I'll explain more about that in a moment.

The first step: save Magic File #1 as Magic File #3. Then consider making these changes:

* Digital book copies mess up the pagination because the front cover (you don't include the back cover or spine) becomes the first page. Also, you will eliminate any blank pages, so the numbers become a hodgepodge by the end of the book.

57

* Therefore, you remove page numbers in the table of contents, the header or footer, and the index.

* In the index you add this comment under Index, "Please use the find key to locate the specific reference pages." Then you delete the numbers but leave in the index words in alphabetical order so the reader knows what you found worthy of special inclusion.

* Since it doesn't matter how many pages the digital version has, this is an opportunity to increase the text font size without financial consequences. So why not make it 12- or 13-point type, probably in the same serif type you used in the bound version? (The text on this page is in 11.5-point Times Roman. Don't make it much larger than 14 or it will take many more pages to print.) Remember, when you increase the font size that will alter your earlier page layouts—that will likely require you to insert and delete some earlier page breaks.

* The same logic regarding color. It matters little whether the text is black on white or pink on red—I'm joking. You can use any color combinations you wish in the e-book, including photos and images—which is why you can see color on page 29 in the e-book version of this book. The drawback with color? If the user is planning to print out some or all of the e-book text, he or she may not want to use color ink—and may not know that he or she can go to "Properties" before actually printing and tell it to use only black and white. (We use color sparingly in our e-books for that reason.)

* Probably the greatest advantage to digital copies is that links can actually be inserted and activated. For example, if I wanted to send you to my webpage in the bound version I would direct you to www.gordonburgett.com. But in the digital copy I would probably highlight the word Web site, go to Insert/Hyperlink/ and type in www.gordonburgett.com where it says address.

That way you could simply activate the highlighted (or under-lined) word in the e–book and my Web site would open up. But that also means in Magic File #3 that you must change the typed out addresses to links, then test each to make sure you got it right and it's still active.

* In Word, the style program is as baffling to us, the users, as it seems to be to other software languages, so it's best to cruise through the text pages and be sure that it says "Normal" in the top bar before the font and size boxes as often as possible. Don't ask why but that seems to eliminate most of the cases where regular type inexplicably appears twice (or half) as large, in *italics*, or in **bold**!

* Sometimes to read your book well digitally you must modify or eliminate your header and/or footer in your e-book.

* We also make our chapter and section heads smaller and uni-form throughout our e-books, so reading the book on a reading device is faster and smoother.

After making all of those changes, you have to go back and read the whole book, at least on the monitor, to see that the layout and contents are exactly as you'd like the digital readers to see them on their computers, on readers, or on some hand-held devices.

When it is ready to print in this streamlined e-book version, save that file as Magic File #3.doc. And hide this file with the other master magic files.

Make a copy of the final Magic File #3 and tell your PDF software to save it as Magic File #4.pdf, for those ancillary publishers who want this electronic version submitted that way.

Again, read #4 to see if it looks like #3. Remember, PDF is particularly pesky at the page breaks, so you may have to do the adjusting here that you had to do with Magic File #2. Ulti-mately, you want Files #3 and #4 to either look alike or acceptably similar. But here you won't have to worry about pagination, the table of contents, or index.

One more niggling thing—and it's very important because it throws a wrench in a lot of ancillary-published e-books.

Some of the e-book ancillary publishers don't want the file in PDF (which preserves artwork much as it is) but they also can't use #3 as it is, in Word. So for them you must go back to #3 and eliminate all artwork—like images, photos, charts, and graphs. Why? Because it simply won't stay where you want it, look right, or somehow not mess up your text presentation.

Kindle is the best (or worst) example. And Smashwords, which saves your electronic book in nine different softwares is a huge roll of the dice. Some look fine with PDF, some are okay in Word, and some look awful in whatever you send.

Again, this is explained more fully in the next chapter.

The real question is, what do you do if you have to delete artwork but it contains valuable information the reader should know? One, you can rewrite the specific section in your e-book File #3 file so the gist of the artwork is explained in printed text. Two, you can simply say nothing at all. Or, three, you say that there was artwork in the bound book version of this text, then send the reader to links that contain the artwork and explain why that was included in the original book. Those links will be at your (or somebody else's) Web site.

Then I would proof this special rewritten version of File #3, make sure it is ready to submit, and I would give it a special title like:

booktitle#3 Kindle.doc

A last look at the cover: magic file #5.

This is a formality. If you have hired out your cover prep, your designer will send you .jpg and .pdf copies of your cover, which you will submit with the text for ancillary publishing.

If you are going to produce your own cover(s) at the ancillary publishers' Web sites, then that is almost the next step on

How to Get Your Book Published Free in Minutes
and Marketed Worldwide in Days

your path to publication. I assume you know what text you want on the back page, you have chosen your title(s), and now you are simply waiting to put all of that into spiffy form to wow eager buyers and readers.

In either case, this is the last chance to review your cover or its contents to make sure it puts the very best face on your prize-winning prose!

Whichever process you use, the cover file is Magic File #5.

Here's a quick box to help you keep the files apart. Remember, when you actually submit your book, you only need two files for each publication, the text copy (for the bound or e-book copy) and the cover:

Final Book Files for Ancillary Book Submission

	Files	Accepted for submission by	Used for
1	title#1.doc	Lulu/bound (prefers .pdf, #2)	Final, ready-to-go .doc format for **bound books**
2	title#2.pdf	Lulu/bound CreateSpace Blurb Lightning Source/ POD bound	#1 saved in final, ready-to-go .pdf format for **bound books**
3	title#3.doc	try at Kindle (*) try at Smashwords (*) Lulu/e-book (prefers .pdf #4)	#1 modified in final, ready-to-go .doc format for **e-books**
4	title#4.pdf	Lightning Source/e-book Lulu Scribd	#3 modified in final, ready-to-go .pdf format for **e-books**
5	title#5.jpg (some accept title#5.pdf)	all—you can also create your own cover in Lulu, Blurb, and Create Space (but not in Lightning Source)	**cover**: usually full cover for bound books, front cover for e-books

The files above are retitled when they must be modified for specific publishers. For example, since Kindle needs format changes, the final file for Kindle, with the changes made, might be called Title#3kindle.doc.

61

Your book is ready to be publicly printed and sold!

Wow! It all looked so easy!

In fact, after all this work many new writers swear off of any such future ventures. They vow to read books, not write them!

That's what makes you so exceptional—you stuck it out.

And you used your head because now you have a set of publishers who will pick up your masterpiece, print or reproduce it, and get it selling worldwide.

That's it—the hard part. The Gordon Burgett system for writing books and getting them ready to pass off to eager publishers, so you can astound that English teacher who tried to switch you to the English as a Second Language classes! Go on, strut a bit: you wrote a real book!

Just don't spend the royalties quite yet. We still have to get those magic files in the publishers' hands. Read on...

Chapter Four

Publishing by ancillary publishers

You can't publish a book until it's written. That's why we've spent our time at Chapter Three and why you have produced the files you will need for publishing.

Actually, the publishing clock starts clicking the moment you have your book saved in ready-to-print form in File #1 (in .doc), plus you have a cover (in File #5)—or will produce one at the publisher's Web site. In minutes you can become a bona fide published author!

How do you do that? We'll show you the step-by-step process in this chapter.

In summary, you simply can take the e-book version of File #1 (either File #3 or more likely your PDF File #4), add in the front cover, and enter it into your respective ancillary publishing site, and in five minutes that book will be posted worldwide for sale! Can it get any faster than that?

What about the bound book? You will submit File #1 (in .doc) or more likely File #2 (in PDF), add in the cover in File #5 (or create the cover on site), and send it to the respective Web site. In a minute or less you'll get back the first proof (you see it on your monitor). You will make any correction or modification you wish until the book is exactly as you want it. When you tell the Web site the book is ready to go, they will charge you to mail a printed proof. You pay the freight, the book arrives in a few days, you approve it, and a few days later that bound book is also ready to be bought by your family, friends, colleagues, clients, or unknown booklovers anywhere.

Again, how can you beat that? All you really had to learn was how to enter files (and maybe a cover) into your computer!

You wonder why those of us with years in the trenches learning publishing shake our heads in awe? (And at the injustice of the time spent learning about picas, halftones, and shrinkwrapping!)

So here's what we will look at in this section:

* who these ancillary publishers are and what printing sorcery they perform on your behalf,
* how you can use them to your best advantage,
* a path I took when I first used them (and why that may make more money for you), and
* most important, how you can best and fastest wend you way through each publisher's submission route, for both bound books and e-books

Ancillary Publishers

Here are the houses (in early 2010) that can put your books in print quickly and free (or almost) and then market them widely. The least exact column is "Your Payment." I used educated guesswork where the amount wasn't clearly stated or possible to calculate with precision. Most paid in 60-90 days.

NAME OF PUBLISHER WEB SITE ADDRESS	PRODUCT TYPE	MARKETING VENUES	YOUR PAYENT (inexact)	SUBMIT FILES IN
LIGHTNING SOURCE http://www.lightningsource.com	bound book	sells your book in P.O.D. format to major distributors, Ingram	30%	.pdf
CREATE SPACE http://www.createspace.com	bound book	Amazon.com, others	20-52%	.pdf
BLURB http://www.blurb.com	bound book	Blurb Bookstore	You set profit above the print cost	.doc accepts .pdf

64

LULU http://www.lulu.com	bound book	own buyers, some secondary distribution	22-47%	prefers .pdf, accepts .doc
LIGHTNING SOURCE http://www.lightningsource.com	e-book	sells to major distributors, Ingram	45%	.pdf
LULU http://www.lulu.com	e-book	own buyers, some secondary distribution	80%	prefers .pdf, accepts .doc
KINDLE dtp.amazon.com	e-book	Amazon, for use on their reader	35%	will convert .doc or .html (sort of)
SMASHWORDS http://www.smashwords.com	e-book	a few major houses	85%	.doc
SCRIBD http://www.scribd.com/	e-book (primarily documents)	sells directly	80%	Windows .doc, .docx, .ppt, .pps, .pptx, .xls, xlsx; Open Office .odt, .sxw, .odp, .sxi, .ods, and .sxc; Adobe .pdf and .ps; wPub; all Open-Document formats; .txt, and .rtf

How you can use them to your best advantage

Ancillary publishing is a business game, and you and the publishers are wise to have your own game plans.

Rest assured that theirs begins with a bottom-line profit percentage that they must maintain to remain in business. They were not created to provide a free production and marketing platform for individuals with books to sell. Rather, that is what they offer so you will select them to publish your book, which they will sell and from which they will retain a sizable percentage of the proceeds. It may cost the writer (that's you) nothing

How to Get Your Book Published Free in Minutes
and Marketed Worldwide in Days

or a pittance out of pocket but what they (you) earn is a modest part of the pie.

The books that ancillary publishers produce must look professional in appearance or you wouldn't choose them nor would others (including distributors) handle or buy them. The books must also be easily and quickly produced—which means that you will do most of the work at the submission level, after having written the book, had it proofed, and designed the cover. You will also create the sales copy, your bio, and take part in their modest promotional efforts—and do some on your own.

The trade-off is that you can have a professional publisher quickly produce a good looking copy of your book in bound or e-book format, post it for worldwide attention, sell it from their Web site, and sometimes link it (in digital or POD form) to other sellers who will greatly expand its exposure to book buyers (though their sales will significantly decrease your income).

What might your game plan be?

If you have never had a book in print, have scant idea how to do it, will not invest the time or money to do it profitably even if the means are explained, and all you really want to do is share some great information and/or have your name in published print to be admired by you and your family and others in perpetuity, you are at the right place at the right time. Who cares about profits? Go for it!

Or if you have one of those high-cost books with a ton of colored photos or high-definition artwork, ancillary publishing may be a divinely-sent vehicle to project you and the contents to fame,

Or if yours is a memoir or a family tree or some product worth sharing but with only a very small circle of fans, bingo.

The same for a novel with a non-celebrity author who has read many novels (one hopes) but has written few or none. If that's you, this is not a put-down. Congratulations for writing a book! But enlist in this army the minute the last word is penned. All novelists start there, and most end there because none of the "regular" publishers will even look at their electric prose.

Am I saying that you cannot earn a handsome return from ancillary publishing? No. But don't mortgage the farm expecting it.

Your game plan may well be that your first book is a learning experience. That means always that the book is the very best you can write, with proper artwork (if needed). It looks professionally designed, has an attractive cover with a selling title and benefits properly placed, and is error-free and logically written (unless it's a novel where logic is discarded). You want to earn well and you will do the necessary promotion so that may happen, but the whole experience is like learning to fly an airplane: it's enough the first time up to get back down safely, with body and pride intact! This is a perfect place to learn to fly.

Or if you are a speaker or performer where displaying your expertise, style, or subject in a professional book will get you more, better, and higher-priced bookings, it is hard to think of a better way to do this quickly than through the bound book ancillary publishers. True, you may buy most of your books to send free to those who might pay you 20 or 50 times more to hear you speak or perform, but that's a smart game plan indeed.

But if you are a published writer with a solid selling record, you are a Web site marketer with a sizable and buying e-list, you already have publishing experience or a firm, or you are an expert (or could be one) in a niche field, you may wish to read Chapter Six later in this book. That will suggest additional game plans in which ancillary publishing might well fit.

I will also suggest that if you plan to live from your writing profits, while an early book ancillary published might make sense, as you progress, ancillary publishing will indeed become ancillary itself. You will be gobbled up by the "big house" publishers (itself, far from a guarantee of big or quick profits), you will empire-build with publishing an integral but supportive

How to Get Your Book Published Free in Minutes
and Marketed Worldwide in Days

part of your earnings, or you will start your own publishing house.

One path you might follow

Earlier I mentioned that to test out this field (after spending nearly 40 years in publishing) I published a book ten times in about 30 days through six of the seven publishers mentioned. (I talk about this in detail in an article in the IBPA *Independent* monthly magazine, see www.ancillarypublishing.com.)

That publishing was done in October and November of 2009. I also revisited each Web site at length and updated the data as I wrote this book in February of 2010.

Let me quickly revisit this experience from a different perspective, one of showing by doing how an experienced publisher might multiply the earnings and exposure that ancillary publishing provides.

Newcomers needn't be confused or discouraged because its approach is different or because its intent is to get the book accepted by every publisher. Rather, it suggests a different reason for expanding into ancillary publishing and, more important, it shows the order in which the publishers are approached and why.

In the section that follows, we will show how one submits his or her book to each publisher. That is divided into bound books and e-books.

This is the path I took. Was it easy to do, as the ancillary publishers state or imply? In most cases, yes, it was. Yet far too often I had to muddle through some cryptic instructions to get anything to happen at all. Most perplexing, there was too little or no help when I got confused or totally lost. But usually it was straightforward. What helped the most was having the five files in final form to insert when requested. Here's what I experienced.

* First, for this live example, I created a book specifically to test all seven formats. It's a concise (110-page) how-to book called *Administrators and Teachers: Getting Profitably in Print 75% of the Time*. I began on day one of the 30-day test (to see if I could get all of the books posted within a month) with the book completely written, proofed, and in ready-to-use layout form.

* I created a core manuscript in Word on a PC, in 6" × 9" layout. (Or you can use a Mac and its word processing software.) What matters is that you do all rewriting, editing, proofing, and text and layout changes in that file before you begin the publishing phase.

* Because my own publishing company will also sell the book directly to clients, retailers, and libraries, I gave it its own ISBN to use on all versions.

* I also had my cover designer create a simple but professional, multicolored cover. He included the ISBN and barcode on the back and sent me the cover in four files—front cover only and total cover, each in .jpg and .pdf format. (Lulu, Blurb, and CreateSpace will let you create a cover with their software, but this is not easy, and options are limited.) Do it my way and if you have multiple versions of your book, they will all have the same cover.

* The ancillary publishers will request book descriptions so I wrote them in advance. This means creating good sales copy that is full of benefits and is reader/buyer-directed. Write two basic descriptions, one about 200 characters long, the other somewhere between 750 and 1,000 words. Then you can expand and prune as space requirements dictate. Also, create a list of keywords related to your book's theme and contents.

69

* I sent the manuscript—in PDF, paginated for book printing—to LSI, Ingram's LightningSource division, to get it digitally printed. I needed 50 fast, bound starter copies at the outset to send both to opinion molders for testimonials and to several niche associations with approaching conventions or conferences. I also sent the full cover to LSI as a .jpg.

LSI sent me a proof in four days. It was perfect. I okayed it, and 10 days later, I had the printed books in my warehouse.

Let me expand a bit here. Because I have owned a publishing company since 1982, the initial 50 POD books are simply part of my usual publishing routine when I need some quick, early book copies. But the rest of the ancillary publishing system that I describe involves a new set of selling venues that anybody with a solid book to sell can pursue—one, several, or all of them—without having any established publishing structure. In fact, some writers may well start with the ancillary markets. Then if their sales cry for the creation of their own self-publishing firm, use the LSI and POD route as the production bridge to help launch their business.

My firm will sell the printed copy of my book to bookstores, libraries, associations, and other niche outlets both directly and through wholesalers, plus I will sell the book in bound form via my Web site and through Amazon (www.advantage.Amazon.com) and Barnes & Noble (www.bn.com). Through the firm's Web site I will also sell books to our e-list, and I will use my blog, social networks, online associates, and other digital means, including AdWords (www.adwords.google.com), to increase those sales.

* I also arranged for LSI to sell my print-on-demand book through major distribution companies, including not just Ingram but also Amazon, Barnes & Noble, Baker & Taylor, and others. In the section that follows I walk you through that process. That isn't free.

How to Get Your Book Published Free in Minutes
and Marketed Worldwide in Days

* Once I had my 50 bound books and that very same book was being offered elsewhere by LSI, I used the same PDF file to have bound books created and sold by both Lulu and CreateSpace. I describe those steps below.

* I didn't approach Blurb in October because I couldn't figure out what it did. For this book, I used its new, much improved Web site description and format to see where it fit into the seven-firm process. I also describe where it excels below.

* Then I took the basic .doc digital file and modified it some for various e-book markets. Most of the e-book intermediaries want my text in PDF format, which I prefer because I can include tables and they will remain intact.

* I arranged to sell through the e-book division of LSI. Once you fill in the forms at the e-book section of LSI, it's as easy as sending your e-book PDF text master and your front page cover file, in .jpg. (E-book publishers only want the front cover, not the document with front and back covers and the spine.)

* Then I went back to Lulu to post my e-book version, though I could have done it (had I been more attentive) earlier when I posted the bound book text.

* Next, as you will read below, I got the book set up for the Kindle. Kindle has its own reader language. PDF won't work, but Amazon will take your Word file and convert it. We'll discuss the problems later.

* Smashwords was next, and it pays the highest. But its value seems to be more that it will translate your e-book into nine DRM-free e-book formats for various readers and apps.

* Finally, I revisited my old friend Scribd, which wants documents primarily but easily absorbs books. See the steps and reservations below.

Where would you end up if you followed this path?

You would have some printed copies of your book for your own use (or for the creation of your own publishing company), plus you'd have an LSI marketing arm selling your bound book (in POD format, printed by them as needed) to major distributors, all in addition to having bound books being sold by Lulu, Create Space, and perhaps Blurb. You'd also have the same book with an identical cover now widely available as an e-book through LSI, Lulu, Kindle, Scribd, and Smashwords.

In other words, you'd have lots of ancillary publishing selling outlets that you didn't have before, plus copies for your own use. The best thing: it's all the very same contents with the same cover.

Enough of me. It's time for you to go Web site wandering, to find the ancillary publishers you want to produce and sell your book!

In the following two sections of this chapter I will tell you who publishes bound books and how to submit your book to them, then the same for e-books.

Some of the process is easily understandable and differs little from site to site. But where sites or segments are confusing, I will linger longer there to help you through the verbal maze.

LightningSource / Bound Books

I use LightningSource three ways.

The first, mentioned but not covered much in this book, is that I send them the files of new publications to print some starter POD bound books while we wait for our rotary (offset) press run to arrive. We often order 50 or 100 books to give out early to antsy buyers, reviewers, and in-field experts to garner testimonials.

But in the ancillary publishing vein, let me discuss how you can use LightningSource (LSI) for your bound book.

You can have LSI sell your bound book almost from the first day in a POD (print-on-demand) format through the major distribution companies, including Ingram, Baker & Taylor, Barnes & Noble, Amazon.com, NACSCORP, and Matthews Medical. (In the U.K., they sell through 11 more distributors that you simply don't have time to access otherwise.) Why is that important, particularly if you don't have an established publishing firm and aren't eager, now, to create that business structure?

It lets you in the back door to some of the largest distributors that are usually unreachable until you are large and have an established selling record. And you may want to avoid dealing directly with many of them as long as possible anyway. Most are imperious, their processes are labyrinthine, they delight in penalizing you if you don't comply to the letter, they can break your bank with their return policies, and they want at least a 55% deduction!

So while your income from LSI won't be much, having them act as your intermediary can be a blessing. Let them hassle with their colleagues. Earning not much—it's hard to calculate your returns, but I'd guesstimate it at about 30% of the

73

book's retail price—is far more than nothing, especially when you literally have naught to do with the marketing and you don't have to print, stock, and ship physical books.

Here's how that happens.

You set your retail price, your discount, and your return policy. LSI lets the big distributors know what you have to sell. They capture the demand from booksellers, libraries, and some consumers and then print your book to match the orders, putting your book in the distributors' hands in days. Your cut? "We collect the wholesale price, deduct the print cost, and pay (you) the balance," says LSI.

Sort of. Their service costs you $1 per book a month ($12 a year). Unmentioned, your pay starts arriving at least 90 days later. And there's a set-up fee and a shipping fee for the proofs, you need an ISBN, and you must provide a finished cover.

One advantage: LSI lists its in-stock total as 100 copies at all times, so back-ordering is avoided. They guarantee that all Ingram's (the primary distributor) orders will be printed and on the shipping dock in 8-12 hours. And if indeed a giant order wafts in (you should be so lucky!), they will switch it from digital to offset printing at quantities of 750 for hardbacks and 2,000 for paperbacks and make it available in 7-10 days.

(An aside: this won't be your best selling path if you sell niche marketed products or to specific product markets that regularly buy in volume from you. But even there, if your spin-off sales are scattered and you'd rather focus on core customers, LSI and the whole ancillary publishing mechanism is a solid way to let others augment your income without your having to become much involved in the process once your book is posted and the proof is acceptable.)

To clarify, you aren't printing books for LSI. You will send them two magic files, they will send you a proof to OK, and you will then join 500,000 "books" waiting to be quickly printed, color cover and all. On a typical day LSI adds 500 new titles; manufactures 50,000 books; fulfills 27,000 orders; serves 9,000 publishers. On average, it prints 1.4 million books a month. In fact, it's the largest distribution channel of wholesalers, retailers, and booksellers.

LightningSource is also the only ancillary publisher where you pay a set-up charge. With my test book, that cost me $37.50 each for the text and cover, plus $30 to receive the proof, or $105. (That's another advantage of ordering a short run of books from LSI for my own company. Usually you pay a set-up fee for your own POD printing, too, but here once it is paid the book can be used for any purpose you wish: POD copies, the bound copy to distribute, or the e-book also included in the ancillary marketing and discussed later on these pages.)

Incidentally, you can simply scan a book into LSI rather than having to reset an earlier book. Get the details from them, but the set-up cost is $75 (plus you must multiply the pages by $.25/page). Add in the proof shipping cost of $30, too. (Alas, it costs $40 to re-upload files when you make changes.)

LSI accepts three kinds of bound books. Trade paperbacks come in 14 sizes, from 5" x 8" to 8.268" x 11.693." The hardcover books are in seven sizes, from 5.5" x 8.5" to 6.14" x 9.21." And the color books come in five sizes, 5.5" x 8.5" to 8.5" x 11."

They have an excellent downloadable file creation guide at the www.lightningsource.com Web site. Let me highlight a few items I found in it that are particularly important to remember.

They only want a digital file that is "print ready" in PDF. They strongly suggest it be from Adobe PDF and that the default be changed from "Standard" to PDF/X-1a:2001 or the High Quality Print setting so that all fonts are embedded. Also, that the page size in PDF be changed from 8.5" x 11" to the correct size you will use in print. You have to submit your file in their nomenclature, too: it must be isbntxt.pdf or as ibntxt.pdf. Where it says "isbn" you enter the 10- or 13-digit number, without hyphens, for that book. (These are all places we have made errors in the many years that I've dealt with LSI.)

The guide also walks you through the cover process. There are special steps for color books (color cover/color text).

Notice that you need an ISBN number for this process, too. That costs $275 for starters since you must buy 10 numbers at the outset. Of course, it's a rip (particularly since they used to be free), but you will probably use a couple of numbers for each book (at least one for the print version and one for the PDF e-book version). It hurts less if you think of each ISBN number as costing $27.50 apiece.

See www.isbn.org/standards/home/index.asp for details.

You won't need an ISBN for the other, non-LSI procedures (with the possible exception of Lulu). The difference seems to be that LSI sells to the conventional distributors who then sell to the commercial or library users, all of which use the ISBN to categorize each individual product. The other bound book publishers are primary sellers, mostly to their own markets. They will provide their own numbers to you free of charge.

Nor does LSI provide a way to produce your own bound book cover, like Lulu, CreateSpace, and Blurb. With LSI you submit a file preferably in PDF on an LSI cover template (they have templates at their Web site to download), though they will accept covers in .jpg, .tiff, or .ps. They want the cover file named: isbn_cov.pdf or isbncov.pdf. If you are designing your own cover (rarely a good idea) or somebody else is prepping it for you, simply read the "b & w book or color book: cover requirements" at the Web site.

We'll go through the step-by-step submission process in a moment, but there are some other points that should be discussed. Some might be reasons why you might decide not to pursue the LSI bound book process.

Let's assume you have a price you'd want to charge the buyer. Say $15.95. LSI lets you pick that retail price, plus the discount and the returns policy. Beginners usually set their price too low, want to allow a "very generous" discount of

How to Get Your Book Published Free in Minutes
and Marketed Worldwide in Days

about 25%, and laugh at letting a firm or anybody return a book.

But in the commercial world you only have so much flexibility with the price—and you might even see that reduced by the retail buyer who only agrees to pay you your price minus discount but might well sell that book below your chosen price on the open market.

To sell the most books, you should consider a 55% discount and a full-return policy.

The middle folk in book marketing usually give the bookstore or booksellers a 40% discount and keep the remaining 10-15% for themselves. Yet bookstores will take a 20% short sale for textbooks and the like, with full returns. So you discount somewhere between 20 and 55%. Rarely will you sell much to middle folk at less than a 50% discount.

Returns are a much disputed box of snakes and a no-return policy may be acceptable to some buyers now and, likely, many more fairly soon. But at the present, any limit on the book's returnability will certainly reduce the number of books you will sell.

Two other points: it's hard to determine your compensation, and it's even harder to determine when your book will show up on retail Web sites or in bookstores.

I made a compensation guesstimate for the LSI bound book business at 30%. But the actual compensation is calculated by a floating formula. Figure the total number of book pages and find Attachment A (details later) to determine the book printing cost. Then subtract the printing cost from the wholesale price: you get the difference. The example LSI uses is for a 352-page 5.5" x 8.5" paperback at $5.48 to print. If the wholesale price is $10 (retail price minus discount), you get $4.52 for each sale.

Finally, when you sign up, it's best to indicate that you want to be paid by direct deposit. You will get a report around the first of each month (wait for at least three months from the first sale) telling how many books you sold and what you earned. It will appear quickly in your bank account.

77

When will the book begin circulating? Figure about 20 days for it to get into the Ingram flow and maybe another couple of weeks to get on most retail Web sites—the latter is up to them: whether they list it, when, and whether they list its availability in 2-3 days or 2-3 weeks. Amazon is the most fickle and may not list the book or include an image. (Don't fret; you are also going to directly submit to Kindle, the Amazon reader people. Those books they always list!)

Let's get your book created and up and selling! Let's go through the steps you will take at the LightningSource Web site, though I must confess that as obvious as things appear there, the LSI Web site can be bewildering. Fortunately, there are direct human contacts who will quickly and kindly lead you out of the wilderness, plus explain specific questions that may arise. A C- for Web site utility but an A for true help, if and when needed.

1. Open up www.lightningsource.com.

2. To get a quick overview, open Site Map on the top line. It will show the ways that LSI tries to help you through the various services it offers, plus the file creation requirements it has. Just know this page is here when you need a specific place to look.

3. LSI has several formats to choose from. Right now you are interested in their creating a stock POD copy of your book (paperback, hardback, or color book) that they will sell to distributors when they receive orders. That's called Print to Order. They will create the ordered copies on demand and pay you later for the sales. Later, in this book, we will discuss their e-book distribution process, which operates in a similar way. You can also buy your own book in POD fashion from LSI (in digital print or offset runs) and, maybe later, you might be interested in their Print to Publisher or Print to Warehouse processes.

How to Get Your Book Published Free in Minutes
and Marketed Worldwide in Days

4. Return to the top line on the Web site and open the yellow REGISTER box. It will open to NEW CLIENT.

5. In the first paragraph it will send you to open a new account. Open that link.

6. While the form's a bit intrusive, get a login name and password and give them the usual contact info. There's no purpose not to be honest in the third section—they don't appear to bug potential customers very aggressively. You probably don't need editing, book design, and cover layout help, if you created the five "magic" files as suggested in Chapter 3.

7. Try out your login. You will have choices: account, library, and orders. (This is where the confusion for me usually begins!)

8. Go to Account. You will see Easy Access (note the Publisher Compensation Report: remember to check whether you are talking about US or UK sales and if your book is in POD or e-book format), Tools, How To's (this is the most important right now), Get Help (they actually help), and My Stats. If you have an incomplete submission, that's what usually appears in My Things to Do.

9. If you want the painful details, go to the Account link at the top of the Account file, then open the Operating Manuals and Contract Documents. That's where you find Appendix A with the set-up and printing charges.

10. You may also want to see the File Creation Guide plus good tutorials. For some reason, to do that you must return to an earlier site (go to Home) and you will see both locations on the top horizontal info bar. This is when you recheck your ready-to-go file (probably #2, the bound book in PDF format) to make certain that you have the PDF properly set and that you aren't using fonts that aren't embedded.

11. Ready to put your bound book in LSI-POD reselling mode? (You actually follow almost identical steps to create the proof to order your own POD copies.) Go to How to Set Up Your Files at LSI at the Account page.

12. This will walk you through the key 10 steps that will get your book created and sold. If you're mailing a scan book, CD, or zip disk, you will be asked to print the packing list to include in your mailing. If you are downloading files, you will get a link box where you enter the file name (see Digital Media Submission form). Submit the insides and the cover. Whew! Now wait for the proof.

13. When the proof arrives breathlessly at your door, open it and read, hoping to find NO CHANGES in your masterpiece. You must OK the proof or send in the corrections (and pay the shipping for another proof)—a powerful argument for taking full care in the original editing, proofing, and PDF switching processes.

14. If you decide that you want to sell this book yourself as well as let LightningSource sell it, just follow the steps at "How to place an order for your books through LSI." That creates no rights difficulties whatsoever. It's your book and you are also letting LSI print and market it.

15. Congratulations, you have the largest distribution system selling your book—better yet, in a hands-off way, where it all takes place elsewhere risk-free in its own time. You just spend the income.

16. Alas, this route isn't totally free (several or many hundred dollars, with the ISBN, setup fee, cover, and proof costs), but it's only a fraction of the cost and time it would take to do this yourself. On the other hand, figuring a 30% return per book, the true cost is 70%. But without LSI that 30%, or your payment, might well have never happened at all. So it's a positive mixed

80

blessing, better and more spendable than no book being sold this way at all.

One more point. Will your book be good enough to get accepted and offered for sale? I asked the help lady whether LSI passes judgment on the books it lists and sells. She said, "I don't think so. I've not seen a rejection in the five years I've been here."

Lulu / Bound Books

Lulu may be the biggest and best-known of the ancillary publishers. If 276,489 traditional books (bound) were published in 2008 (according to the *Books in Print* database), Lulu reports printing 400,000 books that year, in bound or digital format. It has millions of registered users and 2,000,000 site visitors a month—with offices in Raleigh, London, Toronto, and Bangalore.

It may be large but it's not the easiest to use, and of the seven, it was the least cooperative with assistance—no personal contacts and the robots usually sent me to irrelevant Q & A's.

Still, it must be included if you want the perks: complete editorial and copyright control, a revenue split, and a solid attempt to market its books at its own marketplace, through social networks, and retail listings at Amazon.com and Barnes & Noble. (When I checked to see that my one Lulu book was listed, instead I found eight of my books, plus two by my younger brother, another by my twin, and a surprise book by my nephew [who is my graphic artist]!)

What I also like is the spread of books that Lulu offers in unique layout formats: photo books, calendars, cookbooks, and a new and specific Lulu Poetry imprint. It also produces e-books, CDs, and DVDs, and it publishes in seven languages and sells in four price-listed currencies.

1. Let's start by opening up www.Lulu.com. In fact, go to the Lulu Demo > link in the upper right corner and watch the short video. When it's done, click the "Publish" button and see the kinds of choices and decisions that are available.

2. For now, let's take one more overview of the process. (You needn't take notes since I will guide you through the procedures.) Go to the "Books" box, top left column, hit it, then go down the right side of the new page and find "Publishing Tutorials." You only need see "Learn how to Publish a Book" since

How to Get Your Book Published Free in Minutes
and Marketed Worldwide in Days

the second tutorial, about covers, is included in the first. Return to "Books," then go to the yellow link arrow and push "Start Publishing."

3. It will now ask you to select the kind of book you want: paperback (12 size options) or hardcover (2 options). No problem—you want to sell the same basic book fairly widely by many distributors. Let's pick the paperback for now (you can return and do a hardcover book later, though I'd be wary of dust covers since they rip and wrinkle). Hit "Make a Paperback Book."

4. Three choices here. The title. This is the single most important element in selling your book—pick carefully. (You can change it right up to point of creating your proof.) The author? You. But you want to use a pen name? (Really? Why? You're still responsible for what you write.) Then just put in that name, if you insist. There are three authors? Hit the plus sign to the right for more author boxes.

5. Then you are asked how you plan to sell your book through Lulu. If you are limiting your sales to the Lulu Marketplace, pick #2 and use their ISBN for free. (In 8. below, check "Get a free ISBN from Lulu.com" button.) Also, later, once your book is printed, go to Lulu's My Projects page and check the "Purchase a distribution package" to see if their GlobalReach is worth the additional $75 fee. If your book is highly personal, about your family, or your local region, the Lulu Marketplace may be enough.

6. But if you intend to sell the same core book widely (by other ancillary publishers or through your own publishing house), you probably have your cover professionally produced and ready, with your ISBN number and barcode embedded. In that case, check the third choice (Make it public...) and, in 9. below, check the "Add an ISBN you already own" button. For now, save and continue. We'll discuss this choice more in 9.

83

7. The "Choose Your Project Options" page opens. You will select U.S. Trade (6" x 9"), perfect bound printing, and b-w printing with a color cover. That size is a wee problem since many of the other ancillary publishers print in 5" x 8," but the same layout and text will look acceptable on a slightly larger page. If you are using our file layout in Chapter 3 and your model files are for books 5" (or 5½") x 8" (or 8½"), you will need to create a special #2 file now (and a #4 file later for your corresponding e-book.) You might call these modified files booktitle#2Lulu.pdf and booktitle#4Lulu.pdf. While the file is open, add a blank page at the end of your book (or more, so the book is divisible by four). Lulu's rules! Be sure to give the file a quick page read to spot any page layout abnormalities. Finally, on this page, I'm not sure you can rely on the book cost posted. It gave me four different costs for the same specs at 112 pages, from $5.52 to $7.60. Save and continue. (You will get a reliable cost later.)

8. If you chose your own ISBN (6. above), the next page talks about the ISBN—and here's the rub. If you checked the second choice in item 5 above, to use Lulu's ISBN, by their licensing agreement "You are granting publishing rights to Lulu to act as a publisher on your behalf to retailers and wholesalers globally," "Lulu will assign an ISBN to the title and Lulu.com will be listed as the publisher in all bibliographic feeds," and "Lulu will be the sole source of bibliographic data on your book. Lulu will feed data to the U.S. ISBN Agency as well as to Bowker's *Books In Print*® and other industry databases. The data will identify Lulu.com as the publisher." You can stay in the Lulu realm by changing your title a bit, modifying your text some, and you have a new book: theirs to sell. You'll need a modified cover, too, with your new title, one that is 6" x 9" in size. That's easy for your cover artiste to do and can be part of your fee. Be sure to include Lulu in its filename to keep it distinct.

How to Get Your Book Published Free in Minutes
and Marketed Worldwide in Days

9. But if you checked the third choice, in 6, to use your own ISBN, Lulu now has you check a box that "I have not used this ISBN with any other distributor." (Incidentally, while you can pay $275 to R.R. Bowker for a minimum of 10 ISBNs, Lulu will sell you one for $100. Will you have more than this book to publish in the future?) You have no issue if this page will go through with that box unchecked. Or if you used it with other publishers (but not distributors)—check it. But if you have used it with distributors or if you have your own publishing firm and sell through distributors, a dilemma. Worse yet, asking Lulu for clarification is like talking to a wall. So it's your decision. Maybe #8 is the safe path—and stay away from any distribution agreements with Lulu other than the minimal in-house sales or whatever extensions that provides (which is unclear). Remember that if you submit to the many ancillary publishers you will already be widely distributed through LightningSource, CreateSpace, and Kindle—and Smashwords will also make your book accessible by many other readers in their respective languages. Any additional distribution by Lulu of your modified book will be just that.

10. Your next page may be "Using Your ISBN." This refers to the ISBN that Lulu has assigned you (see 5. above). It tells you where to list the ISBN info (on your copyright, or *volta face*, page), where and how it must appear in the barcode on the back cover of your book, and that it will be automatically inserted if you use Lulu's online cover tool. It's best to look at the links on this page and to download and send the barcode to your cover designer if you are creating your own cover.

11. The next page is Add Files. Here you upload your book's contents. Lulu has lots of clear, helpful links on this page. It wants your work in PDF (so do you, to keep all artwork and images in place), but it will accept files in .epub, doc, .rtf, .wps, and postscript, plus .jpg, .png, and .gif. for images. If your file is ready, just upload booktitle#2Lulu.pdf now. (Remember, these are modified files where you told your PDF converter that Lulu

85

print pages measure 6" x 9", and you've made sure that the total page length is divisible by four and the last page is blank.) Find your file in Browse, then hit Upload. Better yet, try "Take us for a test drive" to see what that file looks like. If it's not 100% right, change your file #1 (your original in .doc), resave it in .pdf #2, and try it again—and maybe again.

12. If you are just preparing your files now, the links on this page will be a good guide, particularly those referring to PDF files. You might upload your .doc files first in Lulu, if that's how your book was prepared. If the result is different than you want, convert the .doc files to PDF. Upload the PDF file. If that still isn't right, go back and make your adjustments in .doc, save it again in PDF, check every page to see that everything is the way you want it, change what isn't, save again, check again, and so on (usually 2-3 saves for us), until it's ready. Then load that final, ready-to-print PDF version again in Lulu. If it's accepted, you will see a box (Project Files) saying so on the bottom of this page. If not, it will tell you what must be changed to continue.

13. Next page is called "Making Your Print-ready File." You can see what others will see when they buy your wisdom! Activate the file, and you will be told that your file is complete, with any changes Lulu made in the process. (They also tell you about their in-house formatting services, in fact services to do anything related to your book. Check it out, if interested. But beware of spending hundreds or thousands of dollars for a book that may only earn in double digits.) Hit the "Download and Review Your Print-Ready Interior" link. The file will reach you as a separate e-mail, with the book's interior printed out as it would appear in print. It's critical that you get the book exactly as you want it at step 11 and that it looks as you want it to look at 12 because soon you will pay for a printed proof. That will take about a week to arrive, and if there are still errors to correct, you must repeat steps 11 and 12 and pay (and wait) for a

How to Get Your Book Published Free in Minutes
and Marketed Worldwide in Days

second proof. (Each of those proofs costs the printed price of the book plus shipping, which is about $13.) Save and continue.

14. Cover time! There are two paths here: (1) yours and (2) theirs. The first is where you have completed your own one-piece cover, with front, back, spine, and ISBN in a bar code, probably all in one PDF file. (Ask the cover creator to send you the .jpg or .gif files, plus the same file saved in PDF.) You or your cover designer may want to review these other Lulu pages: "Mandatory Requirements for Distribution" page—look for D1a (the one-piece cover size for a 6" x 9" book is 12.25" + spine x 9.25"; see the template link), the Book Covers FAQ, and the spine width calculator. Don't panic: most professional cover designers already know the design basics, and if you use the Lulu cover design system, which follows, it is built in. Also, tell the designer to add your ISBN and barcode to your own design: 1.833" x 1" in the bottom right corner of the back cover at least 0.375" from the spine and bottom edge. If the retail price is added, it must exactly match the retail price set (later) for Distribution, in US dollars only. Got the file ready? Find the box in the lower left corner of the Cover Wizard called "One-Piece Cover Creator" and open it. It will give the exact dimensions it wants in PDF. If it's a match, find the file in browse, open it, and tell it to upload. If accepted, the cover appears. Bingo, text and cover ready to go!

15. The alternative is to use the Lulu Cover Wizard. It is kind of a marvel, really, and it is far easier to use now than it was just months back. But it's also lots of fooling around with colors and type size and inserting images—and be sure to save at every step or Lulu loves to send you back to zero! (If you get lost, go to My Lulu and open My Projects, then activate that book link.)

16. The pros and cons of the wizard cover. The pro is simply that you can create a decent looking cover free of charge that will be sized to the book you are publishing. Design it on paper

ahead of time, of course, and create your back page copy and select the images. Sharp images, well written copy, and a grabber title will help make the cover work. The con is that however gifted (or tenacious) you are at creating the cover, it will look like an in-house Lulu book cover built on their rather plain layouts and designs.

17. Open up the link at the top right side of the first page of the Cover Wizard where it says "View instructions and info about this step." Hit the + sign to the right to make it easier to read. (You can't print it out but you can bring it up as you progress through the cover-creation steps. To remove it temporarily, hit the "X".) It will walk you through the steps of Changing the Background Cover, Choosing a Theme, Choosing a Layout, Adding Pictures to Your Project Images, Adding Pictures to Your Cover, Adding and Editing the Text, plus Other Tools and Options: how to save your work, undo and redo buttons, zooming and cropping, and reviewing the cover. At the end you will "Make a Print-Ready Cover" and download it to review (much like the interior text).

18. The process is shockingly simple, but you must persevere. Note the "back" box lower right. That's to let you roam frontward or backward. Simply do what the drop-down instructions in the previous section say. You can change anything, resize, use different photos, change the theme and background color— just keep previewing to see if this is the kind of book others will consider professional (if that's what you want) or will buy. It's sort of fun, very limiting, and, of course, Lulu has eager elves waiting to do it for/with you, for pay. When you have precisely what you want, then activate the box on the lower right, "Make a Print-Ready Cover." This will be delivered by e-mail in a few minutes.

19. When you save and continue, you are asked to Describe Your Project. This is very important if you plan to sell any of your books! Pick the most appropriate category (that's where

How to Get Your Book Published Free in Minutes
and Marketed Worldwide in Days

you are listed in catalogs), add as many one-, two-, or three-word keywords you can think of (to let Google and others find your book), and zero in and create a hummer of a 1000-character description (about 100 words; use your word count tool) that makes others drool to see what's on your pages. It must be sharply written and spelled correctly! Insert the language, add the current year and your name in the copyright box, "Standard Copyright License" is fine, and if you are using your own ISBN, put your publishing company name as the publisher. Save and continue.

20. At last, we need to know how much your book will cost you and how much you will earn. The "Set Your Project Price" page has two boxes to check, assuming you aren't giving your download version away free. (If you do, why would anybody buy the printed book?) You can read the drop-down explanation in the link top right. In short, Lulu suggests prices for both editions. You can increase them, and each time your revenue will go up with each sale. But as the price rises, the number of sales will likely drop. At a certain price, sales will disappear. You can also lower them, but you can't go below the combined manufacturing cost and Lulu's cut. If those equal $7 for print, you cannot put the retail price below $7. You also risk, for the printed version, that by lowering prices, the retail markup (which can be half of the retail price) will erase your revenue entirely. (For example, my bound Lulu book, *Administrators and Teachers: Getting Profitably in Print 75% of the Time*, sells at $15.95 elsewhere, but Lulu priced it at $16.01. I receive $7.54 if they sell it internally, $3.54 if sold through distributors retail. See more about the digital download version later in this chapter.) The low profit margin may be a powerful argument for limiting at least your print version to the Lulu Marketplace exclusively. (You can print your bound copy less expensively elsewhere and sell it directly to retailers. No more Save and Continue. Now you get to review your project!

How to Get Your Book Published Free in Minutes
and Marketed Worldwide in Days

21. There it is, your cover and a link to the contents. Time to leap backward (at My Projects) to make any changes. Be cautious about paying right now for marketing help. If the book is a non-seller (many are great books but nobody buys them), all the help won't make much difference. And if it's a huge seller, there's time enough to build on that later. For now, two more things. Create a preview (see the link on this page) and wait for the final word from Lulu before you order a copy of the first edition to use as your proof.

22. You can also find the full review of your book at My Lulu, where lots of other links hide that will help you find, revise, or market your book. Go to Preview and click the edit button. I tried repeatedly to use the "Design your own" line, and when another box appeared, the "Custom page range." Then in the blank box I typed 1, 6-14, to get them to the cover and right to the heart of the first chapter. But it never worked in either the bound or digital books, so I now use the first box, "Simple," which gives the reader a look at 10 pages plus the cover (both covers for the bound book). That's fine. I just want them to see enough of the writing to know it's professional and the book has content they will surely want to buy. The point: activate this preview so your readers will get a bit of the taste.

That's it. The Lulu instructions seem far more confusing if you aren't looking at the Web site text on your monitor as you follow this guide. Persevere!

When the book and cover, and all the related elements, are submitted, and the result is how you want your book to read, order the proof, review it, and give Lulu the okay.

Then you either wait for the Lulu world to find you or you continue on to Chapter Five.

How to Get Your Book Published Free in Minutes
and Marketed Worldwide in Days

Createspace / Bound Books

This is Amazon.com (but not Kindle, approached separately because of their own in-house digital software used for e-book sales). CreateSpace sells your book in bound format.

Think of CreateSpace as a sort of POD wing that funnels your book into production, then sells them primarily through the www.Amazon.com Web site, though it has just opened an "expanded distribution channel" (EDC) that sells, it says, to or through CreateSpace direct to bookstores, online retailers, libraries, and academic institutions. More on this later—it may not work for you and costs more for participation.

The entire layout is clean and easy-to-use, and when I posted my test book (and had the too-frequent first-time minor mishaps), they were prompt in answering questions—with specific answers that solved the issue quickly. The Web site has the feel that the designer actually approached the process like we do, with minimal technical understanding, step-by-step questions, and the need for link guidance every time a new term or procedure was introduced.

There's also some paid technical or editorial assistance, typical to ancillary publishers. It's fairly expensive. Before you contact the respective helper(s) for a bid, you might read https://www.createspace.com/Services/EditorialEvaluation.jsp

Assuming you will be doing the submission process yourself, these are the key details I'd want to know.

1. Open www.createspace.com.

2. On this page, focus on the "authors" section, and return later to the "Expand Your Book's Distribution" and "Community" items on the right. Hit the link "Learn more about our on-demand products" under the word "Filmmakers." When that page opens, link on "Books on Demand."

3. You will open on a page saying "A book to be proud of..." Find a horizontal row of links above "Book features." Look at each of these links before you "create the book," to get a pool of starting knowledge that will make what follows more sensible. We will touch on the highlights.

4. Stay on this page for now. Note that all book covers are printed in full color and CS (CreateSpace) will provide a free ISBN if you wish. Then it shows the three distribution channels available. You will use the first two—and maybe the third (EDC).

5. Open "Sales & Royalties" on that link line. Most important here is what you will be paid every time they manufacture your book to fulfill a new customer order—that's right, there is no standing stock (inventory). The primary determinant is what you set as your list price, because from that they will deduct their share. What is left is your royalty.

6. Look at the two links to the right of "Calculating Your Royalty." The first explains that you must establish the full retail price for your book—if it's for sale through another channel (as is your case, if you are selling through several others, as I suggest). All renditions of your book will sell at the same price. That price should be in the same price range as other, like books offered elsewhere. It must be higher than CS's publish-at rate if you want to earn royalties. And all royalties will be calculated against your list price even if the sales channels sell your book for less.

7. The second link, "How we calculate our share," shows that "their share" is composed of the sales channel percentage (the CS eStore keeps 20% of the list price per sale; Amazon.com, 40%, and EDC, 60%), the fixed charge (see the rates for the standard or pro plan), and (in some cases) the per-page charge (again, standard or pro plan). If, for example, your book is 150 pages, black and white, sold through Amazon.com, standard

How to Get Your Book Published Free in Minutes
and Marketed Worldwide in Days

plan, and you charge $17.95, your royalty would be $1.50 plus $3 deducted from $10.77 ($17.95-40%)—$6.27, or 35% per book sold. The rest is "their share."

8. Let's address the pro plan versus standard. If you're going to use the EDC for distribution, you must use the pro plan, which costs you $39 your first year, then $5 annually for each of your Pro Plan titles. Benefits? A larger royalty share and less cost when you order your own books. Since you can sign up at any time, my suggestion (which I follow) is to wait until you see how many sales CreateSpace makes from your first (and maybe second) book (and how the EDC program is structured and functioning) before spending that money and moving to "pro."

9. Click open the "Pricing" link, which tells you how to order your own books. No royalties on your own books, of course. You will want to check the per-book cost of other POD printers and ancillary publishers and compare the appearance of your book. Also important are any deductions you will receive for quantity buys and shipping.

10. The next link is "Book Sizes and Artwork." Select an industry standard size (14 of the 24 sizes listed), then create a cover the same size. You can build your cover at the CS site (see Cover Creator! linked on that page) or create your own cover as a fully-formatted PDF file. These guidelines are very helpful. Consider using the artwork templates on the bottom.

11. The "Submission Requirements page" on the link line is quite specific. The first three items are where newcomers usually err. Be sure you own or have permission to use the artwork (images, charts, cartoons, whatever), they should be 300 .DPI, and remember to embed all fonts and images in your PDF file. More margin is better than too little, and bleeds can be tricky. Your interior copy must be sent in PDF.

12. The last link, FAQs, is worth seeing, mostly to view "Watch a Video Tour of the CreateSpace Self-Publishing Process."

13. Time to get your book posted! At the top of any page, open Create a New Account.

14. When that's done, link Add New Title on the upper left side. Mostly you will complete the first two boxes along the top: Title Setup and File Review. When the book is ready to go, you will order (and pay for) a proof, and if It's to your liking, you must return a last time to finish Print Ready (which means that others can buy your book from that point forward).

15. The five sections in Title Setup don't require much explanation from me, though I encourage you to pay much attention to the title and description, reworking the latter so it is the most descriptive and compelling possible. People buy books to receive benefits; don't make them guess what they are! Regarding the ISBN, use your own ISBN—unless you are going to participate in the EDC program, in which case you should let CS assign your book one of their ISBN equivalents.

16. Continuing on the Title Signup, only if you have an imprint will you list that here. Pick the most related BISAC category (mandatory). Remember to include lots of appropriate keywords by which seekers might look up your book or others like it at Google.com. The contributors might include the cover and/or book designer, illustrator, and proofreader—and you, of course, as the author. Create an honest and full biography that particularly emphasizes your accomplishments in the field addressed in your book. You will be judged by the description and biography so be sure to get both proofread! Then save what you've done.

17. The next page, Physical Properties, is where you enter the kind of interior type the book has (black and white), the trim

size (I mostly use 5" x 8"), the number of pages (remember that at 110 or more you are charged per page), and the paper color (white unless there's a reason to use cream). It should say "Complete" as each page is saved and you move on.

18. Add Files is next. The page tells you your book's spine size and ISBN number(s) to include in the back cover bar code and in the inside copyright, or *volta face,* page. This is where you upload your PDF interior file. Then you either enter your .jpg or .pdf file—or you can use their software and create your own cover at their Web site. If the latter, link in that box.

19. Let's look at the "Create a Cover" software for a moment. This is a good feature to expedite the process and save money, but the cover will probably look just that way: an amateur's attempt to throw together an acceptable cover. Still, if you go this route (it will tell all at the bar code that it was created in Cover Creator), first hit the question mark in the upper right corner and you will see an useful "Tools Help>Cover Creator" tip sheet. Be sure you know what front cover image, which photo of you, and the best publisher logo (if any) you want to use and where they are hiding in your files. You will also want to write enticing back cover copy—or perhaps front cover, depending on which of the 33 design templates you pick. You can go back and edit. Be sure your text color is strong (or dark) enough to be clearly read and that your colors when used together aren't too bizarre.

20. When the cover is completed, move on to the next item, the Sales Channel Management. (If you are still waiting for your files or mulling over the quick-cover choice, you can close that page.)

21. Here, you might consider not upgrading to Pro, inserting your book's list price (you can change this later), keeping the Amazon and eStore sections enabled, keeping the e-book boxes

at Public and US and international sales, and, for the present, not upgrading to EDC.

22. Now check your Review Setup, the fifth section of the Title Setup. It's really a summary of the other four, so you see what you told CreateSpace (and, soon, the public). You can't get to the second section (file review) until this is acceptable. Once it is, this is where you either submit the files and cover for publishing or you flee (hit cancel, but then you must start the process again).

23. When you hit "Submit for Publishing," CS will look it all over to see that it meets their submission requirements. In the next day or two they will let you know by e-mail whether it's OK or needs changes. If the latter, they will tell you how to update (change) the files. Or that it's time to order your proof. Questions? Open the Book Help link on this page.

24. Later, you will finish the Order Proof and Print Ready pages. It takes about a week to get the printed proof in the mail. Read it closely, and if it's acceptable to sell to both friends and the world, tell CreateSpace. If not, send back the corrections. The only bad news: you have to buy another proof! That's a solid reason for taking your time with the Title Setup as well as the creation and proofing of the interior and cover files.

25. This being an author and publisher is hard work. That's why 99% of your friends will go bookless. Congratulations!

Incidentally, would you like to make a lot more than that 30% or so that CreateSpace and Amazon will send you (actually, your bank, about the first of each month, after several months in their float)? Do it one better. Stay with Amazon and the rest of the ancillary publishers, but also become a publisher yourself.

How to Get Your Book Published Free in Minutes
and Marketed Worldwide in Days

Blurb / Bound Books

This is a different ball game. Blurb has the easiest instructions of all the ancillary publishers, though the implementation at the book-building level is more complex. And there seems a lot less chance of selling your book for a profit here. They feature personal books mostly directed at family or friends.

When I first tested the ancillary publishing venues a few months back, I simply couldn't figure out what Blurb did—or how I could do it, or would even want to. That's remarkably different now. The write-up is very clear, with almost every question answered. Still, I've decided not to post *Administrators and Teachers: Getting Profitably In Print 75% Of The Time* at Blurb for now because I don't see the potential buyers that would justify spending the time and energy needed to re-formulate the text.

But that needn't dissuade you if you want to create a quick book that your relatives might buy and cherish. When might you be particularly interested in Blurb? If you're creating an art book, or where Blurb publishes what it calls QuickStart books: travel, wedding, date book, family yearbook, cookbook, baby book, journal, poetry, and a best friends book.

It's fairly easy to tell where their format seems to work best. Since Blurb only sells through its own bookstore, I looked to see how many books in each category that bookstore had sold (of about 67,000 in total, in December 2009). Of the 35 categories, 11 topped 1,000 books sold. The leading categories (and percent of the total sold) were arts and photography (27%), travel (17), weddings (11), fine art photography (9), children (5), portfolios (4), sports and adventure (3), fine art (3), biographies and memoirs (3), poetry (2), and parenting and families (2).

Arts books constituted almost 40% of the total. The books in business (211) and education (515) were less than 1% combined, and few of those were directed at educators.

97

The emphasis at Blurb seems to be more on quality and appearance than on creating a broad, general-market big seller. They stress commercial and bookstore quality yet have only one selling outlet—unless *you* buy in quantity, then market through other stores.

Blurb offers these six sizes (followed by softcover and hardcover one-book prices): square at 7" x 7" ($12.95, $22.95), b/w text 5" x 8" ($4.95, $16.95), standard landscape 10" x 8" ($19.95, $29.95), standard portrait 8" x 10" ($19.95, $29.95), large landscape 13" x 11" (hardcover only $54.95), and large square 12" x 12" (hardcover only $59.95). The covers at the Web site look appealing: perfect binding and 4-color, 10-pt softcovers, and dust jacket or ImageWrapped, directly printed, matte finished hard covers. Contents can be from 20-440 pages on standard paper or 20-160 on 100-pound text silk-finish paper, either delivered in 7-10 business days.

The actual book price depends upon the number of pages it contains. Using the square (7" x 7") book as an example, see the per-book cost (with four-color printing, minus tax and shipping), on the following page:

There are also volume discounts of 10-15% calculated from the book's base price.

Page Count	Softcover	Hardcover Dust Jacket	Hardcover Image Wrap
20	$ 12.95	$ 22.95	$ 24.95
50	$ 15.95	$ 26.95	$ 29.95
100	$ 19.95	$ 31.95	$ 35.95
200	$ 29.95	$43.95	$ 47.95
300	$ 47.95	$ 59.95	$ 65.95
400	$ 58.95	$ 66.95	$ 72.95

All of the bound book ancillary publishers provide paid assistance if you don't have the time or technical deciphering skills to do it yourself. Blurb's are with outside firms (177 Bound Nation Providers) listed in total and by specialization, ranging from 11 translators and 28 marketing pros to 112 photographers and 121 designers. Other categories are editors, illustrators, image restorers, image scanners, instructors, and writers. If economy is an issue, get bids from the competitors.

One surprise was the Blurb Gift Card, valued from $20-500. What's it for? Buying your book or other books at the Blurb Bookstore.

How much do you earn from a Blurb book? Whatever you want to tack on to your book's price above the book's cost. For example, you might charge $10 for a $4.95 book, which will earn you $5.15—or $19.95 and earn $15. Alas, most of the books are much more expensive—and in fields where you will probably sell nearly all of your books to your family and those who love you! (How many of them will want to pay in the $30-40+ range per book about your baby's first photos or your resort trip to Sisquoc, California?) There's a surprise in the contract, too: a $5 US processing fee every month you receive payment (when you earn more than $25), at which time you are paid by check valid only 90 days from issuance. (Most other ancillary publishers deposit your payment in your bank account, free.)

Blurb accepts no returns (unless a book arrives damaged, with a manufacturing defect, or some defect in workmanship). They are properly emphatic that what you send them is what they produce—you'd better check, recheck, and run a copy on your own printer to check again to make certain there are no typos, grammar flaws, unfinished text, or other text errors; no low-resolution, blurry images; no design or organization errors, or anything else you don't want in print. The same good advice that all the ancillary publishers make, but Blurb is more emphatic about it.

Which leads us to actually creating your book through their software.

Blurb offers two ways to download your book into their software. I'll follow the paths of both, in A and B below.

How to Get Your Book Published Free in Minutes
and Marketed Worldwide in Days

Let's first take path A. It is more compatible with our five-file preparation in Chapter 3. This path involves PDF, actually File #2—although it would have to be heavily modified to fit into the Blurb page sizes. The cover as well must be resized for all size formats, and the book must have an even number of pages.

But if your purpose is to sell your book for a tidy (or any) profit, you may decide to pass up this (A) approach. If your book is personal or for family or close friends, consider the second path, B.

Nonetheless, here are the A steps.

A1. Open up www.blurb.com.

A2. On the first page you are given a choice of opening two formats in yellow arrows. For now click "Use Your Own Program." (Along the way it will ask for your e-mail address and a password.)

A3. On the new page, where it says "Upload Your PDF," go to the first column near the bottom and find an orange "requirements checklist" and click it.

A4. Quickly read that FAQ answer. If it makes total sense, bingo. But, if not, go to the bottom of that answer box where it links to "PDF to Book Publishing Guide" and click that.

A5. Go to the second item in PDF to Book Resource information, where it says "Six Easy Steps to Create a Book using PDF to Book Workflow," and open that.

A6. This is precisely what you have to do to modify your File #1 (your final book file in .doc format); make all of the changes there. Go through the file item by item, particularly paying attention to the text format sizes, then save it when done in PDF. Call it booktitle#2Blurb.pdf.

A7. You may have to convert this new file into PDF/X-3.2002. If so, return to PDF to Book Publishing Guides and go to the next section called "DF/X-3:2002 Export Settings for Adobe® Products" to convert your file into the format that Blurb requires.

A8. Ready to Upload Your PDF? Go back a page or two with your "back" key and hit the Upload Your PDF link.

A9. The rest is fairly straightforward. It will ask you a final time if your PDF text is in downloadable shape. If so, hit CONTINUE.

A10. You will now go through four successive pages: Book Size, Book Details, Upload Cover, and Upload Pages, progressing forward with the CONTINUE button on the bottom of each page.

A11. On the Book Size page, hit the proper response to book size, number of pages, kind of paper (standard or premium), and the type of cover you designed.

A12. At last, your Book Details! Can you sense the finish line? Here you enter the title (and subtitle, if used), author's name, category (you select), a short description (this is important: make the book pop with benefits), and whether it's a public or private book.

A13. There's a mystery item, too: the Blurb logo, which it says will appear unless you pay extra to remove it! Fat chance. But if you use PDF, it seems to just disappear on its own. Free. (Their explanations about this are cryptic. No cost is mentioned anywhere that I could find.)

A14. Here you upload your book cover. You simply browse and enter the file name. (You may have to return to the cover file and resize it to fit Blurb's book page size.)

A15. At last, you enter the book's contents file and send them Blurbward. Then you will receive preflight details as the firm checks to see if what you sent works. If it doesn't, you will be sent error info and instructions about how to fix the difficulty. Their customer support team will help here if the error seems beyond repair—or you can delete the book!

A16. You then get a chance to preview the book. If you remember something you left out, or you want something deleted, you can hit the Edit button to make these changes.

A17. When the text and cover are ready to release, you will upload your book, then order a printed copy to read. (Buy one first to see if it's exactly as you want it before buying a dozen to give away or telling your family to order.) It will take 7-10 days to arrive. Enjoy those last days of pre-publishing obscurity!

A18. Confusing? Despite Blurb's assurances that it's bone-easy, it isn't, at least at the PDF level. But they do have helpful FAQs, video tutorials, and training webinars.

The PDF path is rocky and may be hard to justify among the many other ancillary publishing choices, but Blurb's QuickStart books are a much more fetching alternative, smooth and fun to set up. They can result in the creation of valued lifetime keepers.

The B list that follows applies to Blurb's QuickStart books.

B1. Here, at the first page at www.blurb.com you simply activate Download Blurb BookSmart.

B2. Then do it again, then a third time. This rendition is for PC.

B3. This will produce a download wizard. Answer its questions. Remember to write down the name of the installer (like Google or AOL) where you hide the software; also tell the wizard to leave an icon on your opening screen. This process will end up depositing a zip file on your computer.

B4. When that is done, open up BookSmart on the screen (or go to the installer, find it, and double-click it open). Then click a selected "Blurb QuickStart Book" format.

B5. For this process you must choose from Blurb's selections. For example, let's download the "family yearbook" and create an imaginary book about the kind of family reunion that I describe in my *Your Living Family Tree*. Let's imagine that we gathered in, say, Chicago from all parts of the country to begin an every-decade tradition, as well as to get some videos, photos, and podcasts made of the older members while they were still with us.

B6. While there we took literally hundreds of photos (.jpgs) and had interviews with 16 of the family's oldest members, which we edited into unique snippets 40 to 100 words long. We decided to build a book around the "Burgett Elders."

B7. On the cover we used Burgett Elders as the title, listed the editor, and added an editorial committee of six on page two. We placed the best photos of each of the 16 elders on either the front or back cover.

B8. We edited and saved the best 96 photos in a file which we stored in Documents/My Photos. We opened "Get Photos" and went to Documents/My Photos, where we highlighted all 96 and moved them to the photos layout "table" on the screen to the left of the templates. As we needed them, we simply dragged the appropriate photos to the photo insert boxes on the cover and interior page boxes where we wanted them to appear.

B9. We did the same, finding the 16 bio snippets in a folder in My Documents, then cut and pasted them on the respective pages, arranged from the oldest to the youngest.

103

B10. With one page dedicated to each "elder," we modified the page templates to leave one box for a copy of the cover photo, another for the person's bio, and a few more for photos of the person from younger days.

B11. Play with the categories at the top to select and modify templates. That will let you change the page to some text/photo mix. You can do it yourself, but you can't overlap. It's best to delete what you won't use first, then resize and reposition the remaining boxes before you move the text and photos into them.

B12. It's alarmingly easy to complete your book graphically, and it's fun. But remember that the final book isn't inexpensive. The buyer will properly expect top-quality writing, solid layout, and the very best quality photos. Spend considerable time on both the content and appearance so the end result justifies your time and the buyer's money spent.

B13. Beware of overdoing the designs and background colors. Try to maintain consistency in layout and writing style. Soft is better than harsh or loud. White can be the loveliest (and most imaginative) color of all.

B14. Preview the book regularly. Print the pages on your home color printer to see approximately how they will look in the final edition. (Each home-printed copy will say "For Proofing Only Printed via Blurb.")

B15. When you are ready to roll, tell it to Publish and buy a copy.

B16. Blurb offers good instructions in the four-page Blurb QuickStart Guide.

B17. Since you will be selling this book through Blurb exclusively, there is no reason to use ISBN numbers or many of the

How to Get Your Book Published Free in Minutes
and Marketed Worldwide in Days

other items usually used on the *volta face* (second) page or back cover. Use what you see in other books that you think applies.

B18. What about the copyright? Wait until the book is printed and in absolute final form, then (only if you wish; there's no law that you must) contact www.copyright.gov/forms. Fill in the form, pay the $35 fee, and send two copies of the book to the address provided. (One will be available in the Library of Congress.)

That's it. These QuickStart books can be priceless gifts of unforgettable memories.

Publishing E-Books by
Ancillary Publishing

Almost all of what we need to know about the e-book process I have highlighted in the various publishers' Web sites below, except that there is almost no magic with e-books: they are just the digital file of bound books.

Well, not exactly, because most of the publishers wanted the original text modified to fit into their software pagination and image-reproducing limitations. That often requires adjusting or removing page numbers throughout, including the table of contents and the index. It also requires you to check the PDF files for page-break glitches. And because the reader can directly link references in e-books, you will likely change www... addresses into direct links, which the reader can later activate. Make these changes in your copy of the master .doc file (this is Magic File #3), retitle it, and save it in a PDF file (Magic File #4), which can become your master for all the digital versions to be sold through all of the ancillary publishing companies.

Here are the specific, step-by-step instructions, plus commentary, about submitting e-book info to the respective ancillary publishers.

LightningSource / E-Books

By now you've probably been through the set-up and submission process with LightningSource, your bound book file and cover are in LSI's huge library, and your book is about to be widely sold.

LSI also sells e-books, though our experience (for many years now) has not been very profitable—in the three digits annually!

On the other hand, it really is as simple as taking your #4 magic file (the e-book PDF version), filling in the info and metadata material, and sending the interior (book) and cover (front cover only) files so they can be, alas, very modestly sold.

If you don't have an LSI account, see the instructions in 1-7 beginning on page 85 where I describe LSI bound books. Once you are logged in, open your Account page and find the link "How to set up your eBook files at LSI." The steps for bound and e-books are remarkably similar.

1. In step three you set up the files for which you have titles ready to upload: the Microsoft Reader, Adobe eBook (that's the PDF choice), and the Palm Reader.

2. Step four is the basic metadata information and the subject code or description, as explained on that page. The Parent ISBN is the same ISBN of the print version of your e-book. If it's never had a bound version associated with it, then you just enter an e-book ISBN.

3. It's a tad confusing in step five. This is eBook General Information: the eBook ISBN, price, discount, the Pub and Street Date of your eBook, plus a book description. The DRM stuff is a bit baffling. Hit that link under Protection Level or see the eBook Operating Level and see what feels best to you.

How to Get Your Book Published Free in Minutes
and Marketed Worldwide in Days

4. eBook Territories is step six. If you own the rights, go for the gold—let them distribute your book everywhere.

5. The seventh step is the breadwinner. Here, you will submit, separately, your e-book interior (the book contents slightly reconfigured for eBook presentation) and the Marketing image, which is akin to the front cover. The files can be sent as a file download, on a CD, or in a zip file. The last two are mailed; the first sent by link here.

6. The Marketing Image (cover) here is a 510 x 680-pixel .jpg of the front cover, in 96 dpi. As it says, it should be portrait oriented (taller than wide) and in RGB colorspace. (Frankly, we have just sent the .jpg of the bound cover without much worry about the details and it was always accepted. However, if the title isn't strong and easy to read, you might redesign the cover so it is easily read in thumbnail format in catalogs, which is how it will usually be seen.)

7. Correctly titling your e-book file is very important: for the contents file use the ISBN number, like isbn.pdf; the same for the cover, with .jpg last, like isbn.jpg—both extensions (pdf and jpg) in lower case.

8. For the rest, simply follow the same steps described above for LSI bound books.

If you do it wrong, look at the "My Account at a Glance" section on the Account Page. It will remind you that you must finalize the proof order at the end of the set-up process. You do that after all the steps are completed and you find yourself at the "Titles Not Yet Submitted (Work in Progress)" page.

If, on that page, all the metadata is OK, it will appear in blue. Select SUBMIT from the drop down menu and click Go. If the box is white, you need more or correct metadata.

How to Get Your Book Published Free in Minutes
and Marketed Worldwide in Days

When you click Go, you will be taken to the Review Title Action page, where you must agree to the set-up charges. Hit "I Agree"—or don't!

Good news: there is no set-up fee for the e-books at LSI. And the e-book proof will be sent to you e-mail free of charge.

If you're mailing a CD or zip disk, you will be asked to print the packing list to include in your mailing. If you are downloading files, you will get a link box where you enter the file name (see Digital Media Submission form). Submit the insides and the cover in separate links. And that's it.

One last niggling thing at LSI. It's hard to see what you have sent them and its current status. Here's the solution: log in, go to My Library in your Account section, go to Title Information/Links, then in the Search section insert your name (or the author's) and up pops a six-column info sheet: the ISBN/SKU, Binding, Title, Contributor (author), Submit Date, and Status. It will indicate whether that entry refers to a POD (bound) copy or an e-book (Glassbook).

Lulu / E-Books

There are two ways to post your e-book at Lulu, it seems.

The conventional way is just to let them also sell your printed book as a download, and you collect 80% (or 65.1%) of the income. In fact, this seems to happen automatically if you opt to have both produced during the process. Just check the "download" option at the same time you pick the Lulu (bound) book option, then later price that download version differently. (I set the download price at $10, a little under 2/3 of the bound book price.) I presume they send the buyer the very same book, as a download, minus the back cover.

But I wasn't aware of this the first time I posted my Lulu book so I must not have made the "download" choice when given the chance. Anyway, I had a separate, easier-to-use (by the reader) e-book text file and a front-cover only file—and I wanted the e-book to be uniform wherever it sold. So I went back to Lulu to post my e-book version, and I had a far easier time because I'd already navigated the Web site maze.

When I opened "Publishing" on the site I did see that you could just add information about your e-book to the information about your bound book. There was a related link to do this, I think, but it didn't work. So I went through the full process again, this time inserting my booktitle#4.pdf e-book file for the download. (The book file size at 5.5" x 8" didn't seem to matter.) At the cover, I went directly to the text insertion box and put in my PDF version, which worked fine. (This was my #5 file, actually in .jpg, which I converted to PDF and saved as bookcover#5Lulu.pdf.) The rest was easy.

There was no question about ISBNs nor any comment that I couldn't distribute this version through others, so I checked any box that discussed sales by Lulu, distributors, and anybody else who wanted to buy or hawk my words!

The only other thing I did was let viewers take a preview look at 10 pages of the e-book, as explained in the Lulu bound book information above.

How to Get Your Book Published Free in Minutes
and Marketed Worldwide in Days

There is some question about the amount I will earn from my digital book version(s). When I first posted my e-book, I priced it at $10, and Lulu said that $8 would be mine on each sale. (Which is how it still reads at My Lulu listing.) But in recreating a Lulu test copy for this book, it now says "to account for hosting and transaction costs, we had to add a base price of $1.49 if you collect a creator revenue; however, if you want to give your download away for free, Lulu will wave this base price." In other words, if you want to get paid, off comes $1.49—I think. I'll see when the sales checks arrive. I'm not banking on Lulu's (or any other publisher's) e-book sales to amount to much, frankly. Still, 80% (or 65.1%) of that may pay some small bills...

Kindle / E-Books

Kindle has the best known e-Reader program. They are part of Amazon.com and are eager to include your books to be read on their reader (or through the Kindle system). Inclusion costs you nothing—well, nothing more than a headache trying to get your book to read right.

It's one of the most problematic sites because it uses its own quixotic reader language, PDF won't work, your files and charts and many images are unwelcome, and you are either caught having to adjust and retry your copy until almost all of it looks good, pay someone else to do it, or just throw up your hands and send it in as close as you can get it and hope that the readers are patient.

On the surface, it's simple: you just send them your original ready-to-go .doc file, #3, and they will convert it from there. If it were really that easy...

Sometimes it is. Half our Kindle books have been converted without problems.

But too often—and the test book that I used for this ancillary publishing venture was no exception—goofy things happened: the text is squished or twice as big (and bold!) or pages break mysteriously. And all tables and almost all images must be expunged—left in, they are a disaster.

My solution with the expunged data is to send Kindle readers to a Web site page of my own where they can see or download the graphs, charts, or artwork that appears in the original book and on most other ancillary publishing versions of this product.

Do you want to see an example of that? The test book was *Administrators and Teachers: Getting Profitably in Print 75% of the Time*, but in the Kindle version I had to delete the artwork. I sent those readers interested to my file of the same artwork at www.gordonburgett.com/kindle.htm.

If you encounter distressed Kindle text copy, you have some choices, since Amazon's directions for preventing oddi-

How to Get Your Book Published Free in Minutes
and Marketed Worldwide in Days

ties are pretty awful for the non-techie. You can start there, nonetheless, if you are well versed in HTML: see "Modify Converted Copy" where you upload your file. Pay particular attention to the mysterious Word style formatting. Try to get your book as much in Normal style as you can—check to see in the toolbox where the type font appears at the top of the Word page. An alternative is to hire an elance.com or guru.com helper to apply magic (for about $50–75).

Is there a way to see what the book actually looks like once it has been accepted, with or without a Kindle reader? Yes, Kindle software is available free for PC, but you must still buy your own book at Kindle to review it!

Any recourse if you know or suspect it looks less than acceptable by your terms? You can unpublish your book at any time.

A final thought. At http://jakonrath.blogspot.com I stumbled on a rare revelation while researching this section, an excellent blog (Oct. 13, 2009) by a professional writer, Joe Konrath, in which Joe talks about his actual earnings from Kindle. Joe suggests that e-books priced at $2 sell an average of 4900 e-books per year; at $4, 1100 books, and at $8, 342 books. That the biggest profits are from the lowest-priced books.

Let's walk through the Kindle e-book posting process.

1. Before you send your book to their converter, make the changes in your .doc file that you would make for other e-books. (Thus it becomes your Magic File #3.) I mentioned most of the changes above: mostly adjusting or removing page numbers throughout (including page numbers in the table of contents and the index), checking for page-break glitches, modifying or eliminating your header and/or footer, making the chapter and section heads smaller and uniform throughout, and directly using active hyperlinks. Also, since Kindle won't accept PDF format (despite what it claims), you might reduce if not remove the artwork, too: the images, charts, graphs, and other things that will otherwise float around on your pages, unan-

113

chored and apparently unwanted. Save this modified file as booktitle#3Kindle.doc.

2. Now head for www.dtp.amazon.com. (That stands for the Digital Text Platform.)

3. Fill in the boxes on the upper left to create your Amazon account. If you already have one, just use your e-mail address and that password. Don't go to the Community Forums yet. You will be back with questions later—or to the FAQs above. (If those fail, the only place to get any human Kindle response seems to be at DTP-Feedback@Amazon.com.)

4. Go to "Getting Started and FAQs," where you can either Browse the Knowledge Base or go to the Forums.

5. Time to plunge in: open the "Getting Started Guide." Assuming you have ready-to-go files, you're going to post your book and cover, hold your breath, see what the book looks like, then probably return to the Formatting Guide.

6. Listed on that page are the five most important places you must know about. (You can find them at any time at "My Shelf.") You already have an account, so go to Publish Your Content.

7. Read the contents titles on this page (you may want to read them in depth later if you have specific questions). Start on the fourth item, "Start Here to Publish Your Content."

8. You must complete the four items before you can successfully push the "Publish" button near the bottom, at which time everything disappears for a day or two—no editing or buying.

* Do #1, "Enter Product Details." The instructions are clear here. You don't need an ISBN number, but if this book has one, use it. Titles are critical: choose carefully, and make

certain that the readers know exactly what they are buying by what you call it. You want to provide the potential buyer as much information as you can, so either use your prepared description or create enticing, benefit-laden copy in your description that makes the reader say, "Wow, I need to read this right away!"—and write that in comprehensible, concise, correct English (or the language the book is in) so they see that you are indeed a good writer. Don't use "enterprises" in your publisher name (too enterprising) or anything else that hints at madness or a con. You can use that date as the publishing date, the form helps you select categories and authors, and you can leave the three boxes to the right of the Product Image empty. That leaves the cover.

* It's far preferable to have a colorful, appealing cover. People do buy books by the cover—and title. All that's needed here is the front image. You can use their Amazon's Product Image Guidelines, if needed. Prep the cover in .jpg or .tif. It must be at least 500 pixels on its longest side, but preferably 1200 pixels or more. Don't panic if you make a mistake—you can correct it now or later. Kindle isn't very helpful but the process is forgiving. When done, save it. You can return!

* Boldly continue to #2, to Confirm Content Rights. No mystery here, unless you stole the copy! You only have an issue if you entered other agreements (probably with a publisher who "bought" the print rights). Find out if the electronic rights remain totally or partially yours. Only in the latter case must you pick out the territories where the rights are yours—discuss this with the other person or firm, and, if necessary, get a clarification in writing. Otherwise, select worldwide rights, check the box that confirms that you can upload the content, and go to #3.

* The next section is where you will find (browse) your book file, upload it, and see what it looks like (or should) when Kindle publishes it. The instructions here are well

115

written so just follow them to put the book to the test. A couple of advisories: nobody I know ever got PDF to work in Kindle, and the .html will drive you daft if you're a novice. The best approach is to make all of your changes in Word first, then simply save everything in one .html file (rather than .doc) and submit that as your final copy.

* What's left is the list price, from which you will earn 35% per sale. This is what you think others will pay. You may want the full $200 Kindle price cap (you must charge at least $1), but if nobody with reading ability (or sense) would pay more than $10, that's tops for you. (Remember the blog comment earlier that the lower the price, the greater your sales.) Anyway, Kindle seems to freeze what they charge for many book prices at $10 (our book, selling at $15.95 through the ancillary publishing markets, sells for $10 at Kindle). Put something down: you can change it whenever you wish.

(9) You're almost in print! But you must hit the PUBLISH button first—if you have filled in all of the required items and checked the right boxes.

You're Kindled! Check your information at Amazon.com: just hit "books" and your name. You're famous. Money? Soon, at the end of each month, modest payments will start appearing in your bank account. "Royalties" may be overdoing it, but well deserved nonetheless.

Another modest bank deposit.

How to Get Your Book Published Free in Minutes
and Marketed Worldwide in Days

Smashwords / E-Books

Here's a unique service that has lots of potential, is well designed, is fairly easy to use, and pays a relatively whopping 85 percent of net (book price minus PayPal fee times .85). It also has other earning outlets which could mean more income.

Moreover, the honcho, Mark Coker, has written two free, straightforward guides that are enlightening, humorous, and helpful. See *The Smashwords Book Marketing Guide* and *The Smashwords Style Guide*.

First, let me explain what they do as a free digital publishing platform and e-book distributor, with their tools for digital publishing, marketing, sampling, selling, and distribution.

Smashwords accepts your File #3—your e-book file in Word (.doc)—and converts it into nine DRM-free e-book formats: .EPUB (the open industry format), PDF (the best for fancy formatting and artwork), .RTF (rich text format), .PDB (mostly for Palm Pilots), .MOBI (Kindle), LRF (Sony Reader), TXT (plain text), plus the online HTML and Javascript. In other words, it uses what Mark calls a "meat grinder converter" that translates .doc stuff into the other languages that are needed to be read by all of those other e-book readers.

That's the beauty and the beast. The beauty is that it opens literally millions of possibilities that your words will find their way into others' favorite reading tools. You can pay others to convert your book for you, one language at a time, but it isn't cheap. Or you can let Smashwords do it free—and it isn't perfect, as you will see when you review the formats (at least those you can) once you have posted your book. Some of mine looked great (PDF, TXT, and HTML were the best). Others looked tortured when read on my computer through Word. Maybe they were perfect in the right digital tongue!

But you can reduce the switchover absurdities if you do as Mark says:

"DO NOT upload your book until you've implemented the recommendations in *The Smashwords Style Guide.* Smashwords reserves the right to remove poorly formatted books."

I never saw the checklist when I sent in the #3 file—and found my book in limbo (worse than removed, just sitting there) until I made several of the style changes suggested, re-sent a special #3 file, and got a quick OK. What would I do now? Look through the *Guide* first, quickly, to see which of the sins I was committing, upgrade the file, and send it in. (I think my upgrade took about 75 minutes total.)

Here's the process:

1. Open www.smashwords.com.

2. Go to the bottom of the first (left) column and download the *Style Guide.* I did it in PDF. Or just read it on your computer by opening the HTML version.

3. Save a copy of File #3.doc and make the changes on the copy that are most likely to clog the meat grinder. Then save the "corrected" copy as title#3smashwords.doc.

4. Go to "How to Publish on Smashwords" and read the clear explanations.

5. Near the top of the webpage you will see seven categories, starting with HOME. Go to PUBLISH and open the page.

6. You will be marched through eight steps, which you must complete before you hit the PUBLISH box at the bottom.

7. In #1, type in the TITLE (and sub-title) of your book. Next, insert your short description, expand it to a tad under 400 characters, and proof it, under SYNOPSIS. Mark the LANGUAGE

OF THE BOOK and whether it will offend young eyes under ADULT CONTENT.

8. In #2, indicate how much you are charging for your book: free, the readers decide, or a specific amount ($ .99 minimum). In SAMPLING, it's a good idea to let the Smashwords visitor see some of your book free. It can be 10%, 35%, 50%, from page one—you pick. It's fair game, too, to discreetly refer once or twice to much-sought items that are found on pages after the free section!

9. In #3, simply pick the most appropriate CATEGORIES in the boxes that appear.

10. #4, TAGS, one to a line (I entered 13), help potential readers find your gem by key words they regularly use.

11. Why not check all of the conversion formats indicated (unless there is a reason not to) in #5, e-BOOK FORMATS?

12. It's far better to use a COVER IMAGE than not, even if it's plain. You can upgrade #6 later. Make sure the title is clear, easy to read, and well balanced. Your name as the author (without "by") also appears! You must save that image in a .jpg, gif, or PNG file—the resolution isn't important. The file must contain less than 20MB.

13. Here's the BIG DEAL in #7: your book! Insert your ready-to-go file, title#3Smashwords.doc (or title#3.doc). It can also be in .rtf. Maximum file size, 5MB.

14. The last step, #8, is to read the PUBLISHING AGREE-MENT, which you accept when you tell Smashwords to PUB-LISH your book.

How to Get Your Book Published Free in Minutes
and Marketed Worldwide in Days

15. Then wait for the acceptance, which comes quickly—unless you blow it the first time, as I did. They take a day or several to get the file in a workable order.

At some point Smashwords will snag you to complete your account file info, your profile, your payee information, and other wee intrusions. They are easy to do. In fact, this may be the best of the fill-in processes in ancillary publishing.

Three things I particularly like at Smashwords.

One is an affiliation system, where you can make your book accessible for affiliation sales (although that reduces your income to 70.5% per book). Why not, to get lots of others offering your book for sale through their blogs, Web sites, or newsletters? It will tell where and how affiliates sign up for access to your book(s). They earn an 11% or more commission of the net sales price.

Two, Smashwords has a coupon program where you can offer discount (or free book) incentives to prime your sales or to attract selected buyers for a limited-time offering.

And the third, Mark's vision of somehow using your books on YouTube, though that is not explained at any depth. Presumably it is linked back to Smashwords so enraptured viewers can instantly buy.

They also offer a $150 service (through Wordclay) to format your book, if that's beyond your skills or patience. Or if it's just a good economic decision so you can get on to writing other books!

Two other things in Coker's *Style Guide* are particularly worth sharing. One, since it seems to apply to all ancillary publishers: what Smashwords publishes—and doesn't. They want original works direct from the author or the exclusive digital publisher. No public domain works (unless by the original author), incomplete or partial books, or books that appear elsewhere on the Internet under other authorship. (They also

How to Get Your Book Published Free in Minutes
and Marketed Worldwide in Days

strongly discourage get-rich-quick "systems" for making money on the Internet.)

The second is a list of the "Five Most Common Formatting Mistakes." They are (1) improper indents: "don't use tabs or spaces for paragraph indents"; (2) repeating paragraph returns: "never use more than four or five consecutive paragraph returns"; (3) font and style mistakes: "don't use fancy, non-standard fonts; large font sizes over 14 points, or multiple paragraph styles"; (4) table of contents: in your e-book "don't include page numbers in your table of contents or index"; and (5) copyright page mistakes: include the required "front matter." Additional Smashwords' headache-causers? Text in tables, columns, or text boxes; automatic footnotes; text wrapped around images; automatic indexing, and WordPerfect.

How to Get Your Book Published Free in Minutes
and Marketed Worldwide in Days

Scribd / E-Books

Scribd sits a bit at the side of the other ancillary publications because it primarily deals in documents and short books—average length publication is 43 pages (13,640 words). Charging for your document or book also seems to be at least tacitly discouraged. Their selling mechanism also seems the weakest of the seven.

They seem big on sharing information. Scribd provides the platform to write and make your words available, presumably to draw readers to your area of expertise and thus validate you as the authority. You write, upload, and either make the text accessible or sell it through the Scribd bookstore, which is also rather hard to find. But if you do sell something, your profit ratio is high—80%!

What will they accept? Information, novels and novellas, factual essays, poetry, newsletters, original sheet music, resumés, corporate reports, presentation slideshows, recipes, and more. They don't seem to care if the cover is a plain old black-and-white term paper front page or fancy and multi-colored. Nor is an ISBN an issue or whether you are sending the same text to other publishers.

Most ancillary publishers accept your book in just one format (or two), but Scribd excels in taking your offering 19 different ways—see the comparison chart on pages 64-5. Getting it posted could hardly be easier, though if you want to change items (like a cover, which is the first page of your submission), you must resubmit the entire manuscript or document; and once a copy has been sold, that's it, no changes. The original will remain posted, and you can then submit new versions.

As different as this publishing vehicle is, you can't just dismiss it. Scribd claims to be the largest social publishing company in the world, visited by 60 million viewers a month. Begun in early 2007 in San Francisco, it includes items in 90 different languages and has posted more than 35 billion words.

How to Get Your Book Published Free in Minutes
and Marketed Worldwide in Days

A hidden plus: they don't care if you link back to your own newsletter or blog site.

I posted four items at Scribd on 6/4/09: two free, two for $3 each. I listed "101 Niche Marketing Ideas" in two categories. In about six months 645 have opened it at business/law and 308 at how-to guides and manuals. The two paid items have lured in only 195 and 93 viewers—but not one sale, at $3! How could 60 million monthly have missed such gems?

My conclusion, comparing all seven ancillary publishers and having dabbled with Scribd, is that the better your description is here (and almost everywhere else too), the better you will fare. The title had better grab the wandering eye, too. Otherwise, there's a mountain of free things for the picking at Scribd and it's easy to get lost or overlooked. The point: see other titles and descriptions and work hard to make yours as appealing as possible.

I'll give you the submission details in a moment, but if you want a good model for a short book that I liked, see Sr. Genaro Medina Ramos' *Náhuatl* course book (that's the language spoken by the Aztecs). Complete, concise, full of content, and well supported with explanatory information.

Here's the submission process:

1. Open www.scribd.com. You're in when it has Home, Community, Explore, and Upload along the top line.

2. Go to that upload button. There will be two options. The blue upload is for sharing or uploading items. If that's your choice, there are two checked boxes: Standard and Public. They are probably what you want. If not, you might explore Enter Text or Single File. (The HELP/TOOLS on the bottom will guide you well too.) Then just follow that path...

3. Above the blue choice is the yellow shaded box telling you that that's the road to the Scribd Store uploader. Click the "Seller's Guide" link and you will see five reports. Browse the first two, if you wish, but the third (Signing Up), the fourth

(Preparing Your Content), and the fifth (Publishing Your Content and Configuring Sales Options) will walk you through the process for items you want to sell. The first two have short but excellent You Tube videos that tell you what to do.

4. In the first of the last three, Signing Up, you must open a Scribd account to sell there. Fill in the usual stuff—all the asterisks. If you have a PayPal account, they pay you that way. Or you can be paid by check. You are reminded that your work must be original—but that doesn't mean exclusive.

5. In the next, Preparing Your Content, some of the advice is standard e-book stuff: avoid numbering the pages, 12-point type minimum, keep your margins consistent, and strive to make the content clear and attractive. To keep the final viewed (or downloaded) document consistent with what you see on your computer, they prefer you use PDF, particularly with artwork and if color is used (which they advise against since monitors see colors differently). Shorter documents are best done in list format (8.5 x 11 is fine) but longer books (read side by side) work better with narrower layouts. Very important: test all hyperlinks first since only active links will work in your final e-book. Remember to fill in all title and author metadata. Finally, no passwords or encryptions permitted.

6. The last of the items, Publishing Your Content and Configuring Sales Options, leads you backward to the yellow box you went to in #3 above. Where it says "Click to Chose Files," do that, then find the e-book file (probably #4) you want to download in Scribd.

7. But don't upload that file yet because in Scribd the first page of the file is your cover! So you must, in essence, put #5 (the cover) in the document as page one, add the text (#4) next, re-save it all as one file in PDF, and that becomes your special Scribd file.

How to Get Your Book Published Free in Minutes
and Marketed Worldwide in Days

8. This will be the front cover only and it will be seen as a 1" x 1.5" thumbnail. If your regular cover is fancy, simplify it, keeping these things in mind: (a) color is fine but keep it sharp, unmuddled, (b) use lettering that is clear and easy to read; use a bold sans-serif type font (like Arial), no script, and (c) avoid a drop shadow or special effects but put a thin line outline around the cover.

9. Now, when you browse, find your special Scribd book file, click OK, and a white field will open to the right side of your screen. Follow the instructions there. When you are at the end of several sections in this white window, up will pop your file downloaded and ready to sell!

10. The first section is the download. It will also ask you to pick a price (or let Scribd do it; nothing for less than $1). Close that section.

11. Copyright verification will appear. Tell it how you happen to be selling the copy and give it an ownership reason (like, "I wrote it!"). Hit continue, and in the third section you give the book or item a category, as many keywords as apply, and a description. It will suggest a "discoverability rating" so those 60 million monthly will see you. If it's "low," keep adding legitimate keywords and more description.

12. When you leave that section, you are published! Your e-book (or e-document) is ready for instant selling or sharing.

13. This is the oddest of the ancillary publishing Web sites, the quickest to use, and most likely the least profitable. But being a published author could hardly be easier. And who knows how many of those viewers will wander over to your Web site and buy one of everything you sell.

125

When you publish a book, it's the world's book.
The world edits it.

Philip Roth, 1933-

126

Chapter Five

Marketing your book
the ancillary way

The intent of this book is tell you about the wonders of ancillary publishing, help you prep a book to publish quickly and inexpensively that way, explain the seven publishing choices, and walk you through the submission steps of each.

Marketing your book is something else.

You may not care much about your book's marketing. Sure, you'd like to see your book sell a million copies so you could spend the rest of your time enjoying the profits—who wouldn't? But in reality you'd be delighted just to see the book materialize in first-rate form with your name prominently displayed as its author. The rest is fine if it happens. What a kick if it sold widely to the public or to libraries, better yet, people who know you, particularly those who never, ever thought you could even write!

Or you may recognize the integral role that marketing plays in your book's well-being and will go at least part of the way to promote your book so it might be widely available, seen, and bought.

And you may become a marketing maniac intent on putting your book in every bookstore and on every e-book reader, driving it to the top of its Amazon best-selling category list, maybe even making it become a classroom textbook or required reading.

Marketing guidance

On these pages I will highlight the promotional and marketing means made available by the ancillary publishers, send you to their Web sites for more specific guidance and key links, and let you use their guidance to expand your own selling urge.

I'm also going to suggest 23 ways that other publishers use to better and more prominently position their book to both increase its sales and to enlarge the awareness by others of their expertise about the book's subject.

A stark truth in the small-scope publishing world we are exploring is that books alone do not a fortune make! (I know, "What about so-and-so who made $50,000,000 from a tiny book?" If that happens to you, I will buy this book back from you for double its price for my being wrong—if you will include your full autograph in the mailed request!)

Mostly, the reason you want your book widely known and sought (beyond ego inflation) is that it will earn you far more money by related means—see the list of those means below.

Some of that prominence (initially book-driven) can happen through the ancillary publishers, and that's why this chapter should be read closely and their help should be used fully. It can happen more widely if you simultaneously use several or many of the ancillary publishers. And more yet if you also create your own publishing firm and focus more fully on promotion, enhanced by empire-building—as explained in the chapter that follows.

More thoughts about marketing and promotion

Books simply don't sell themselves. Somebody has to get the printed words in circulation and make the books available to be known of, distributed, and sold to those who want to buy what you say.

When you're a one-person shop with uncomfortable coffers, that somebody putting it all in place is you. But if you (also) sell through ancillary publishing, and you reinforce that through the venues they suggest and facilitate, that can multiply your promotional effectiveness manifold.

As well, there are excellent books that can reinforce your sales campaign if you use the long-tested, more traditional selling methods they explain. As said earlier, I particularly like

Dan Poynter's *Self-Publishing Manual*, plus John Kremer's *1001 Ways to Market Your Book*. Also see Dan's second edition (Volume 2) of the *Self-Publishing Manual* for more web-based vehicles.

Also, don't overlook a different, far less risky, user-driven approach—niche publishing—where, through pre-testing, your core marketing is ready to launch the moment your words see print.

So let me put on my long-time publisher glasses and look at your role as a new ancillary publisher to see where your efforts and time might be best employed for maximum marketing and promotional effectiveness.

Actually, the most important reasons that others will buy your book have little to do with the follow-up marketing or promotion. We have already addressed most of them earlier. This is a good time to reinforce their critical role in making your book sell well. They include:

* the book's **title** must tell the potential buyers that they should read its contents
* its title and cover must at least imply the **benefits** the book's contents will bring—or the **needs** it will meet
* its **cover** must look professional and clearly display the title and those benefits/needs
* the book must be **thick** enough to at least suggest that it is worth its price, but not so thick it will scare off those who must read it
* the book's **price** must be in line with its perceived or imagined content and benefits
* the book must be **well written**, fully proofed, reliably researched, look like other bookstore books inside and out, and contain information, a story, or a supported theme
* the **experience** of reading the book must be positive and worth the time, energy, and cost required

Said differently, if you are writing a book that you want others to buy, you must create a book that shouts to be bought. It must be printed in a professional-looking manner. Find something worth saying, and say it well. Never underestimate the value of a title that captures all in "let-me-at-it" prose, and make the cover exude class and provoke irresistible curiosity.

Ancillary publishers provide professional-looking books. They expect you to have the knowledge, the words, and the skill to submit two core files—the book's contents (including artwork) and the cover(s). If what you provide them meets their expectations, they will likely produce your book. All seven will gladly sell your book, and most will as eagerly get it into other distributing hands.

Sometimes that's all the marketing that's needed. The book catches fire on its own. It has a gilded, rare life where planned marketing is really just printing fast enough to keep up with the demand.

But for the rest of us, the other 99%, at the outset our flame will flash a bit more brightly (particularly when we tell family and friends), it may even erupt into a wee blaze with some additional fevered fanning, but unless our book has one or several dedicated champions it at best will make us a family hero, a local notable, and a spot-filler in some libraries, but in publishing annals we are still all but unknown and unrich.

You must be the primary and most dedicated champion of your own book! At fire starting and fire fanning you must be as good at promotion and marketing as you are at writing and layout, a true and dedicated Renaissance person in a post-Renaissance world. Fortunately, this new world includes ancillary publishers to help and the tentacular World Wide Web! The leverage can be yours if it is exercised with vigor and incorporates the wise use of the new tools at hand.

Yet, as I noted above, your first, best selling tools are that great title, that eye-catching cover, and a captivating subject and text! Every hour spent creating those is worth many hours

How to Get Your Book Published Free in Minutes
and Marketed Worldwide in Days

later spent trying to explain what should be obvious—why your book should be bought right now!

Additional marketing and promotional tools

A fast look at the many ways you can promote your book on your own first, then a more detailed review of how the specific ancillary publishers help you promote your book through their means.

1. **Description.** As we mentioned earlier, you need at least two super introductions, each self-contained, that tell what your book is about, its purpose and the benefits it brings, plus why it is unique. One is short (100 characters); the other is long (750 words). Expand or contract if you need something in between.
2. **Biography**. Who are you to write this book? What singular knowledge, experience, or skill do you bring to these pages? What in your background or experience led to this uniqueness?
3. **Two-sentence sales summary**. Called the "elevator speech" among speakers, it's the "wow!" summary you give between floors in an elevator when somebody, in this case, asks, "What's your book about?" Make it tight, conversational, benefit-heavy, and quick. Then learn it cold and do it with a smile!
4. **10-20 bullet points** of compelling contents. Write them; then prioritize them in order of interest and value to the potential reader.
5. **Web site.** Build a Web site that complements the book, or your expertise, and house the book and everything else related harmoniously on its pages, with every facet of the book and you accessible by link.
6. **Squeeze page**. A short one-link page to either your shopping cart to buy your book or to your landing page, which also has one exit, the order form.

131

7. **Landing page**. This picks up from the squeeze page, sells in greater detail, promises benefits and needs met. To see an example of both a squeeze page and a landing page, see www.gordonburgett.com/6-7link.htm.

8. **Empire-building**. If you're an expert about your book's topic, create more books that are linked to it, and also more related products by other means, all accessible through your Web site, integrated promotion, and your newsletter/e-list sales. If your readers will "buy more products from this great source" (that's you), create and sell them, with your Web site the hub. (Empire building is what my free newsletter is about. See www.gordonburgett.com/nl.htm.)

9. **Google presence**. Will your book and your Web site pop up first when you type either (or your name) into the Google search engine? That's the goal, to get a million eyes looking your way—plus some buyers. Strategic keyword placement is involved. Are keywords embedded at your Web site? Is your book on the Google Book Search database? See http://books.google.com/support.)

10. **The gadgets.** Some of the ancillary publishers create widgets, banners, or buttons. If they make sense, incorporate them into your marketing. Every time your book is mentioned you want the reader to be led to an information and buying source.

11. **Market close to home**. Don't forget the most obvious (and perhaps the longest suffering since you've been on your book-writing quest): your family and friends—and their friends, and their friends... Of course, those closest to you get a free copy (that you pay for), but if you won't fix their toilet free, they pay.

12. **Testimonials**. If your book looks good and says a lot, the readers will want you to succeed. You can simply ask those who congratulate you if they will send you a testimonial that you can put on your flyer and at your Web site—will they also tell their friends about the newest baby in town (your book)? Make sure they agree that you can use it on all

promotion for your book. If they are leaders in your field and/or wield much influence and have a regular mailing to their clientele, give them a free copy with all of the promo materials.

13. **Flyer**. This can be a bit expensive but if you have ways to effectively distribute fliers to those likely to buy your book, think of getting 250-500 four-color one-sided fliers, with an ordering contact or mechanism on it. Then distribute them!

14. **Social networking**. What's the value of being in Facebook, My Space, LinkedIn, or any babble group if you can't brag (with facts) about your newest creation and how your electronic friends can find out more (at your Web site) and tell others? They might actually buy a copy, or a dozen for their reading group. Who knows? Surely, they have a lonely aunt to whom they can boast about their book-writing friend. It's also smart to tie into the ancillary publishing social networks that will share your new book with others using their services. In that case, send your new friends to buy from the ancillary publisher.

15. **Niche base**. Who most benefits from your words? Here's where you create the magic list of people like you, who share a burning interest in your topic. They buy your kind of book, and they know other fans or fanatics. For example, if your book is *The Ten Chess Strategies Every Player Must Know*, chess is the common denominator that defines your niche beneficiaries. So create (or find) the list of chess information buyers. It tells who wants to know what you know and are sharing in print. Let your mind wander; list every group, person, association, related beneficiary (math teachers, chess stores, specialty gift lists for the gifted), and so on. Then you go to Google and see what more comes up when you enter these in chess+___ (chess+math teachers). A big buying world suddenly becomes yours!

16. **Blog**. Do you have a blog? While it can be free (check www.wordpress.com), it takes time to do right, and it may not be worth it simply to create and maintain just to sell one

133

book. But if you're into your topic for the long run, through a blog you can meet lots of like-minded friends who share your subject in common (like fellow fig cookbook readers, members of the Skylzy family, or autograph traders). If you go this route, read up on how you can make your blog popular and sought. Why not contact www.reddit.com, www.Digg.com, and www.Stumbleupon.com,.

17. **Press releases**. But what about the millions (or hundreds) of others who woke up this morning itching to own a book about the very topic that your book is about? You can prepare a brief (one page maximum) press release that tells the who, what, why, where, when, and how of your book, plus how the editor or reader can find you for more information or to buy. That's where the Web site (and your phone number) work best. (Two free, very popular p.r. services are www.pr.com and www.prleap.com.) Also, check the Lulu PR information below; then download their link "How to craft a strong Press Release."

18. **Articles**. As long as you've written a whole book, why not break it into sharp, short (500 to 800-word) articles and either query and sell them to magazines in your field or submit them to the e-zine article distributors at www. ezinearticles.com and www.articlesbase.com? In your short bio slug, be sure to link back to your ancillary publisher and/or your Web site.

19. **Booklet**. An example is easiest to see. I sold lots of copies of *How to Create a Great Second Life* and also gave many speeches about it. A booker suggested that if I created a 24-page booklet to give to each speech attendee, her association would buy them for $4 each. It was a boon and we printed thousands, which led back to new surges of book sales—and many more speeches.

20. **E-list**. Are you keeping the name and address (plus the e-mail info) of every person and group you are contacting or who buys your book? Then saving those as an e-list? That makes selling your second book or other products about

five times easier—and if you catch the web marketing craze, you will have a responsive starter e-list.

21. **Newsletter**. If you want to cull a following, particularly if you have an e-list, the best way to stay in touch is through a short, informative, free newsletter, probably sent monthly.

22. **Radio and TV**. Since you're sufficiently informed and articulate to have written a book, why not keep going and share what you know on radio (discreetly plugging your book, too) or TV (send them a .jpg file of the cover to put on the screen). Talk shows are the best. Let them know you are available and how your topic might interest their audience. If interested, send them a copy of your book plus related printed info.

23. **Workshops, seminars, or speeches**. Why not convert your book into how-to workshops or seminars to offer to clubs or associations or through college or university ed programs (see www.setupandmarketyourownseminar.com)? Then sell your book as part of the registration fee or as a back-of-the-room gem. You can easily outearn the book's income in a few months of presentations and continue doing so for years.

24. **Audio CD or DVD**. Many books lend themselves to audio CD or DVD programs. Once you have the book, it can fairly easily be converted into a script, and the content can be both oral and a downloadable workbook. (See www.createyouraudiocds.com.)

Let's see what the ancillary publishers offer or suggest, to expand or build on these marketing suggestions.

135

LightningSource Marketing

Frankly, it's all marketing at LSI. If there's no demand—no orders coming to them—they won't make a POD copy of your book and send it to the distributors to sell. And if buyers don't request the e-book, all of the 0's and 1's just sit there in digital netherland, unsold.

So you must do several things to directly help them help you.

Within LSI's confines, you need a selling—usually benefit-laden—description that makes a buyer hit the order key. Yet to get them even to read the description, your book needs a selling title and, in some cases, a first-rate, eye-grabbing cover before they even scan the description. Those are what LSI sends to the distributors, booksellers, and buyers. The title, cover, and description provoke the buying zeal.

The more promotion you do, the more interest is generated, the more buyers ask to see your book, and the more booksellers are going to put it in their stores or catalogs, feature it, and do your marketing for you. Add social networking (like Twitter, Facebook, and LinkedIn), blogs, related newsletters, and other web marketing to that and your numbers will increase at every selling venue, including the obvious ones that LSI supplies.

All of this is particularly so when you don't have your own publishing house. You have no direct means of selling in quantity, so you must direct interest to the traditional book-buying venues (like Barnes & Noble and Amazon.com), so they will seek others, like LSI, for their supply.

136

Lulu Marketing

Lulu has lots of visitors to its site and a ton of folks have produced books through them, so they are a marketing player. Thus I was surprised that the marketing guidance for the publisher was so hard to find at the Web site.

The best things I read were on the "Services" page reached through "My Lulu," lower far left, under "Free Marketing Tools," where it discusses widgets, storefronts, web buttons and banners, Google book search, weRead, media, press releases, the Lulu Marketplace itself, optimized search, social networking, and writing communities—mostly the self-marketing tools and fonts I just mentioned as among the most profitable ways to make ancillary publishing work for you.

Let's focus on three items particular to Lulu here—its storefront, weRead, and the IntrepidMedia—and encourage you to check the other links if more help is needed.

Lulu's storefront is fun to play with and a good place to display your books, so why not spend a few minutes and get it set up to look good. In truth, though, it already exists once you publish with Lulu (mine was there when I first looked) so all you really need to do is to give it a better theme look and insert your contact info. If your book is a serious part of your earning, you need your own regular, clean, appealing Web site where you can post (and link) anything you wish, including your Lulu book(s) and all of your other books, reports, CDs, newsletter, and support information. Using the Lulu Web site as your only one is far too restrictive, but set it up anyway, particularly if this is the only version of your book or you are wedded exclusively to Lulu forever.

Check out www.weRead.com. Being on these pages can give you a much broader presence with your book, and in it you can build a "one author page" for lots of contact services, including Lulu (its owner), Facebook, Bebo, and Twitter. It's a shot at three million book readers. Post the usual bio, your photo, and reviews, plus parse your book into lots of intriguing

137

excerpts that will prompt the visitor to want to read more. It's free and you're mixing with a good crowd!

Then take a quick look at IntrepidMedia.com as a place where you can rub literary elbows with other writers, though I doubt you'll sell much that route. But who knows? If your columns are fetching and you stick to your expertise...

Another good way to "hear" those using an ancillary publishing format is to check their forums and groups. To do this in Lulu, open "Community."

Forums tell you what's happening, what works, and what doesn't at that site. For example, on the Spanish forum, on 1/1/10, it was all gripes about the higher Lulu publishing costs in euros. At another, shouts of praise that the writer's just-out photobook was up and wildly received at Christmas. There are currently 35 active archives, with six in non-English (French, Italian, Spanish, Dutch, Portuguese, and German). About a half million folks have used them. The most frequently visited is "Paperback, Hardcover, Ebook & Brochure Publishing," with "Shameless Promotion" not far behind. When you have a question, gripe, or idea to share, post.

You might check Lulu Groups as well. There are 3,492 of them (including some zero-person groups). The five biggest are Promote Your Book (5,056 members), Creative Minds (1,679), Literary Knights (747), Follow Your Path (742), and Photography and Digital Design (671).

You might also be interested in the Lulu Newsletter and the Lulu Blog. And if you're at Facebook or are a Twitterbug, there's a direct link there, too.

Finally, at "Services," Lulu has folks to help you with your marketing. My thoughts? The profit margin is so low and risky here (really, at all of ancillary publishers) that you should probably exhaust all of the free sales venues or means first, while you get a sense of the potential buying appetite for your book, before you pay others to help you bring even more buyers to a winner.

Createspace Marketing

Amazon.com is anything but a wordless recluse when it comes to marketing, so it is encouraging to see CreateSpace focus on how you can lure potential buyers to find and purchase your new book. They even suggest you actively tell your writing world, niche world, and friends of friends of friends that you have the last word now in print! What a concept!

Two good places to begin drawing buying attention to your book are the "Videos/BookOverview" and at the Community sections of their Web site. The video is promising but the Community section is just more social networking: blog, profile, forum, a brag post (your photo and info about you), and more. Plus a Twitter link. It seems in-house structured, which isn't destined to sell many of your books to those outside the club.

Blurb Marketing

Not much big-market selling here, though the tighter-focused books about weddings, family reunions, vacations, and other family or group gatherings could muster up scores or hundreds of purchases through the Blurb Bookstore.

And, of course, the editor or those closely linked to the book themes will want to tell everybody else who cares that the book exists. The usual social networks, family letters, and newsletters probably do that best.

These may be the prettiest of the ancillary publishing publications but it's hard to see how others would know that they exist lest it be by some viral word-of-mouth and sharing-of-copy procedure.

Smashwords Marketing

Let me refer, again, to *The Smashwords Book Marketing Guide* by the firm's CEO, where much said applies broadly to the ancillary publishing industry as well.

Mark Coker confesses that most books don't sell well, particularly if the author doesn't do much of his or her own marketing. And that e-books are but a small (though the fastest growing) segment of the book selling industry.

He then explains how his firm helps "you leverage the power of digital publishing to reach your readers." How does Smashwords help market your book "without you lifting a finger"?

Traffic (seen by thousands of web browsers daily), Profile page (on the web page created for others to see your bio, photo, blog, books, and a link to buy the print version), Book page (each book has its own web page where viewers can see the cover, YouTube book trailers, and a synopsis, plus read samples and post a review), Sampling, Integration with Stanza and Other Mobile Reading Apps (2.5 million book readers on Apple's iPhone have access to the Stanza catalog to download your book), Distribution to Barnes & Noble and Fictionwise, Search Engine Optimization (making you accessible through search engines), Coupons, Book Reviews, Embeddable You-Tube Videos, Book Tagging, Tag Clouds, Links to Your Other Books, Integration with Social Networking and Social Book-marking Sites (like Twitter and Facebook), Shopping Cart and PayPal, an Affiliate Partners Program, and Promotion on Smashword Satellites (30 specialized micro-sites).

This is a good checklist to use to compare the marketing outlets and venues offered by the seven ancillary publishing firms.

Other suggestions about how the author can promote his or her own book, from Coker's *The Smashwords Book Marketing Guide*:

* Create a large social network to foster word-of-mouth selling of your book(s).

* Use hyperlinks often to let potential readers-buyers know of the book's and author's existence and accessibility. The wider the links are spread, the greater the relevance to the search engines—and the higher the person's listing (meaning that the information is more likely to be on the first page and thus be seen).

* Include the book information in the author's email signature.

* Put your book's existence and selling location(s) at your Web site and blog, with active links.

* Tell your family, friends, and business connections. Send them an e-mail with all the exciting information: title, a quick description, the active links, and a request that they share it with their friends...

* Post a notice at your social networks, including the online communities, LinkedIn, any message boards you frequent (or should), and Twitter.

* Promote each of your books in the others and include an "about the author..." bio in the back of each, with active links in all.

* Create a press release (even a press kit) and circulate it locally, to interested associations, and through free PR wire services.

I would add to that, if appropriate, the creation of a free monthly newsletter in which you can offer information pertinent to your topic and expertise which you send to all those interested through their e-list addresses. You might use Constant Contact (very inexpensive and easy to use) for list man-

How to Get Your Book Published Free in Minutes
and Marketed Worldwide in Days

agement and newsletter mailing. It's appropriate to modestly mention your book and its buying links regularly in the news-letter.

Scribd Marketing

Not the social hub of publishing, although you can tell Twitter and Facebook about your activities here with one click each.

It has an array of badges (see Community): small, profile, button, and incline ("View my documents at Scribd"—then the logo) to post on Web sites or webpages. You can create the usual profile and people can comment about your documents or book. (I'm not sure the Scribdfolk report buyers are particularly chatty.)

One thing you can do is change your price as often as you like, and you can see all viewing and buying activity daily. It's all in plain view, too, at your HOME page. And they aren't afraid to let you broadcast your web pages or newsletter link.

.

Chapter Six

How Can Established Publishers Best Use Ancillary Publishing?

Let's think this through together because if you are an established publisher now, that's the first question you must answer anyway. And if you aren't but you are about to publish, if you stick with it, soon enough you will be established—and it's a valid question at every step of your growth.

An "established publisher" in the book context means that you have published at least one book, probably many. It implies that you have already written or acquired the book text, styled the book, had it proofed, developed a cover, bought the ISBNs, and so on—or at least know how to do that. In short, created the text and cover files and either produced a book in bound and/or e-book format.

Further, without guessing your process or to what degree you have progressed, you also have some promotional and marketing procedures that have made your book(s) accessible and buyable, directly or through other selling venues.

You already produce and sell books. That's exactly where new authors would like to be, too, except that they don't want to have to flail in the publishing world. They seek ancillary publishers because the latter will get their hands dirty with printing ink.

But why would you use ancillary publishers to do the same thing you are already doing now?

Two fundamentally different kinds of publishing

We should distinguish two kinds of publishing at the outset because the answers for each differ.

145

One let's call "**standard publishing**." It's the kind of publishing we customarily think of when an ink-on-paper book is produced. It's the kind that Poynter describes in *The Self-Publishing Manual*. It produces books that are sold to bookstores, libraries, and clients. It also uses distributors to sell the same book widely. While most of the books it produces will be in bound format, they can also be published digitally.

Its most characteristic distinction is that its marketing process finds the book's buyers after the book is in print.

Ancillary publishers do precisely the same. A pair of files is submitted, a book emerges, and the book is strung up the web flagpole so viewers can buy it, while, in most cases, information about the book's existence is also sent to distributors so they can further spread the sale, in POD or e-book fashion.

The other kind of publishing differs little in the book's printing arena but it reverses the marketing order, which in turn directly affects the content, purpose, and preparation of the book that is printed. That's "**niche publishing**."

It starts by identifying and qualifying the book's user—in fact, it even questions if a book is the best way to sell to the user.

It then takes a sample body of potential buyers and asks them if they would buy the product (let's assume it's a book for our purposes here) and how much they would pay before the book is even written or printed.

A typical niche marketing test might send a one-sided flyer, an introductory note, and a stamped return envelope or postcard to, say, 180 or 500 buyers in that niche (like optometrists, speed readers, bank presidents, or mystics). The flyer will include a content pitch, the title, an abbreviated table of contents, the author's bio, benefits, the size and length of the book, its price and format (cloth or trade bound book or e-book, usually), and an ISBN number.

If enough say they will buy the book at "x" rate, and if the extrapolation of that buying ratio is projected against the full

146

buying universe, the question is whether the profit from that sale, after the book production and marketing costs (usually by direct mail) are deducted, will be high enough to print the selling flyer and the book. (A small second test is often conducted to double-check the first results.)

There is more to this process but this isn't the book to fully expand on it. See my *Niche Publishing: Publish Profitably Every Time* (www.nichepublishing.org).

The point here is that the risk factor is largely eliminated in niche publishing by the pre-test, which verifies before the book is written that the sizable costs of niche marketing will be handsomely repaid by a hungry market eager to buy that tested, very specific information that focuses on their unique needs and interests.

Said in another way, niche publishing only happens when the risk is minimal—and ancillary publishing exists, in part, because the costs otherwise incurred in publishing one's own book are also minimal (or none at all).

Thus it makes sense (and saves cents) to expand on these paths separately to see how publishers established in each can best use ancillary publishing—if they can at all!

Ancillary publishing in a "standard publishing" world

I've been a "standard" publisher since 1982, of scores of books of my own and many more for others. And I've produced the same book six times by ancillary publishing. How would I use the latter to increase my income and sales spread?

Let's reduce (and over-simplify) book publishing to three processes to more clearly describe each—preparation, production, and promotion.

For the **preparation**, I wouldn't change a thing. I'd still focus on creating the same two files, the book's contents and its cover. Once those are done, I would modify the content file to condense the style some and save it in PDF so I could sell my book as an e-book. And I'd modify the cover file a bit, too, since I'd need only the front cover, in PDF, for an e-book.

In other words, ancillary publishing isn't an issue in the preparation phase. It only begins once the book is ready to print.

For **production**, I could submit my two most appropriate files to most of the seven ancillary publishers and let them produce the book. I could even save some production time and money by letting Lulu, CreateSpace, or Blurb create my cover by using the software at their sites.

When might I do that?

* If I have a test book on which I don't want to invest a lot of time and money, bingo. I'm thinking of a manuscript (probably by another author) that I think might have promise. I might do the editing early, have the author read Chapter 3 in this book, have her bring in the final draft in file-ready form, make the adjustments, create a cover, and let the ancillary publisher produce the final bound and e-book versions. If their book catches fire, we will also produce a version of the same book and market it through our already established channels. But I'd keep it alive at the ancillary publisher(s), too, and I'd get the author to use her social networking means to boost sales as well.

* If I have a book that clearly falls outside my primary marketing channels. I wrote a fun book called *Treasure and Scavenger Hunts* (www.gordonburgett.com/scavenger.htm). It was a true orphan on my list, and despite fitful marketing by me, it has been a sweet sinecure for decades. But now I would publish that book through one or several ancillary publishers, and I'd push all promotion their way, plus use all of the marketing tools they have available.

* If I have a novel to publish but my house is non-fiction (or, I suppose, the reverse). Keep your eyes open. My poor, lonely

novel, *Lian McAndrews and the Perfect Human World*, has been hiding among books for K-12 administrators and dentists for so many years it may have fled! It's my next venture (after this book) in the ancillary world. Why? As much as I love the story, it's a bird in a fish world. Let them make the profits and incur the toil.

For **promotion**, I might do things differently—if it were possible to separate the three elements.

Here's what I have in mind. I would love to let all of the ancillary publishers have a crack at a book—that means going to all of them and submitting the same content, the same cover (my in-house design), and the same ISBN (where needed). Then I'd let them do their promotional magic (if any).

If I saw life on the frontier—they are still very much the frontier—I would take that same content and cover file (and ISBN) and I'd either print the book in a sizable rotary (offset) run or I'd have enough POD copies produced (through Light-ningSource) to do a decent in-house promotion, too.

I would let them continue selling through the distributors (though I would also submit the book myself through Amazon Advantage), but I would crank up all of my established market-ing means, too, which would include my own e-list, my news-letter, and, of course, any speaking and back-of-the-room sales I could create.

In other words, I would let them attract their world of buy-ers plus do any secondary buying they want—and I'd develop more buyers through my established means.

That means that I would pay particular attention to the sell-ing tools that I provide the ancillary houses. I'd create the very best description, bio, and other items they request or use.

The one question that remains unanswered concerning the ancillary publishers is how profitable they are for me? In the future that will dictate the best balance that I'll want between my in-house production and promotion and having my own product in competition through ancillary publishers.

149

Once I see the kind of returns they bring me on a monthly basis, then I can better evaluate the kind of savings in time and cost I can make by letting them produce and market my book(s).

If, for example, they bring me half the amount of return that I would normally produce, it might make sense for me to completely switch to ancillary publishing if I can create three books through them in the time it takes me to produce one on my own.

There's another slant, too, for "standard publishing."

Let's assume that you are a new speaker and your topic is "closing commercial real estate sales." You've been a realtor for some years, know your field, have a reputation for ethical dealing, and are a dynamic, content-rich speaker.

Alas, you're a so-so writer though you have a first-rate message, with lots of anecdotes and hands-on stories.

My advice? Write a short book that every commercial real estate winner needs to read and keep on hand. Find a good re-writer or editor to bring that copy up to the level of your presentation. Have a sharp, professional cover created, get an ISBN, and head to an ancillary publisher to get that book out in a week or two.

In the meantime, line up the ten best "dream" speaking gigs you can find, get your Web site press and booking kits in top order, and contact the bookers of each of those programs. Send your book to him or her by mail or e-mail, with an appealing cover letter, telling why that audience would benefit from your message.

While you are shooting for the best bookings, take 50 more of your books and use them to create local or regional speaking programs.

You will buy your own books, at say $7 each, to give away to get $1,500 or $3,000 speeches.

In other words, rather than becoming a publisher, you will let others do the grunt work while you gather and create the copy for the first, and many other, books. Then you will use those books to get speaking presentations—at which you may sell more books to your enraptured listeners.

Where's the profit? Mostly it's in and at the speeches! In the meantime, your ancillary publisher may well be selling lots of your books, too.

If the book is a run-away, a big moneymaker, then read the previous section, get a rotary (offset) or POD run where the per-book cost will be far lower, and lay in your own stock. But in the meantime, let the ancillary houses do best what they do, and use that product to bump yourself up the pay scale by having professional products at hand.

Ancillary publishing in a "niche publishing" world

Using ancillary publishers doesn't work nearly as well for niching. In fact, it hardly works at all.

One reason it doesn't work well is that the per-book cost to you is fairly high from ancillary publishers.

But the most important reason is that their marketing means aren't the same as yours.

If you are producing a book for candle makers, they will simply list it and hope that candle makers might see it—or they will sell it to distributors who primarily sell to bookstores (brick and web) where it will probably be stuck somewhere a candle maker might be expected to go.

In niche marketing, you can't afford that imprecision. You want a top-selling flyer full of benefits and inside jargon plunk in the waxy hands of candle makers. The way you do that is by contacting the extended list of those you test against, a direct mail list of confessed candle makers.

You want to get them to return the order form (or order on the computer, iPod, phone, or whatever they are using now) so you can immediately mail (or e-mail) them a copy of your book. The cost of the book itself is a key part of your profits.

151

* Having said all that, you can do the pre-testing, submit the book to ancillary publishers, and let them have a go at it. But at the same time send the #2 and #5 files to LightningSource, get some POD copies of the bound book for your immediate needs, and quickly (if the PODs sell) send the same files to a rotary (offset) or even a digital press and get a bigger run to sell from your firm.

* You can even do that on a much smaller scale to test a niche market without the pre-testing. You print 150 POD copies and you mail an enticing flyer to 1,500 niche folk on a direct mail list to see if they will buy. (10% is not an uncommon selling ratio if the niche is tight and the book is wanted.) You can buy those copies from Lightning Source or the other ancillary publishers that produce bound books. But check the cost of the book at each site first.

Would I do either of the above? Maybe the first, never the second. The idea in niching is to position yourself as an expert in that field, to create a valuable must-have book at the start, and then add related, needed books or other products as you empire build. The initial testing tells you if the path and topic you are pursuing is really wanted with that title, in that format, at that cost, and as you describe it before you invest much time and money in the book. So much of your money and time goes into the pre-testing. The production is much quicker once you have the files ready, and the marketing is pretty much sending a great flyer to the grander universe that already told you they wanted to buy what you are producing. To me, it makes little sense to poke into niching this way. It and ancillary publishing don't really mesh well.

A reiteration as a last thought. One can think macro here if you're already up and running as a publisher. That is, do what you do already, and when your book is ready to go, spend 10-15 hours and also post your book with all of the ancillary publishers who will have you. Then all of you slug it out in the

152

marketing world. The result? You get random (maybe big) checks and bank deposits at the end of each month from the new kids on the block who are selling your masterpiece in odd places by odd ways that you otherwise would never have sold to anyway.

I believe that it is my job not only to write books but to have them published. A book is like a child. You have to defend the life of a child.

George Konrad, 1933-

Chapter Seven

It's almost a miracle...

The purpose of these pages is to help you see your ideas and words in print quickly and inexpensively without having to become your own, and the only, printer and marketer.

You can submit your book to as many of the seven ancillary publishers as you wish. They will produce a book in hours and sell it worldwide in days. You can focus on the writing while they professionally produce a book that you will be proud to have on display and sale.

Together, with the publisher(s), you can then make your book sell, and sell, and sell.

Even better, you can use the existence of your book to sell you as a knowledgeable, articulate, published author who can speak, perform, teach, or create, all to increase its earnings and to validate you as an expert about its topic or message.

Just seeing your book often in the places where good books are sold enhances the positive word-of-mouth and sales. Sitting on one ancillary publishing Web site is a great start; it means you did the tough stuff right; you wrote a book that can sell. But getting it out to lots of sellers in lots of good-book locations—as much at Web sites and on social networking outlets as in bookstores—is how you can sell your book in volume. Alas, small volume is the only way to create large volume. It starts with you pushing uphill to get enough selling traction to begin snowballing down the sales side... Ancillary publishers are a great place to begin.

If you are new to publishing, to be able to publish your book quickly, well, and with very, very little or no out-of-pocket expense, that's just a hair short of a miracle.

If you're already on the track, ancillary publishing lets you run the same race many times simultaneously or on many tracks at the same time. Or it means that you can let somebody else create comely books from the great copy and cover you provide.

Mostly, it's the first timers who win doubly big.

If that's you, huge congratulations! In hours or days you will be a published author! Your great-grandkids (and maybe your grandmother) can read your book from cover to cover. You're an in-print somebody. Your book will prove that almost forever.

About the author

Gordon Burgett currently speaks nationwide about three topics, "How to Get Your Book Published Free in Minutes and Marketed Worldwide in Days," "Niche Publishing," and "How to Plan a Great Second Life," offering keynotes, break-out sessions, and workshops at conventions, retreats, and colleges or universities. (See www.gordonburgett.com.)

In 2009, Gordon published *Administrators and Teachers: Getting Profitably in Print 75% of the Time*. In bound and/or digital format, it is available from Gordon, Amazon.com, lulu.com, lightningsource.com, createspace.com, smashwords.com, and as a Kindle book. (For details, see www.ancillarypublishing.com.)

In late 2009 and 2010, Gordon also released specific products about how to publish ancillary publishing books. Those were combined, updated, and expanded and are the core of Gordon's newest book, *How to Get Your Book Published Free in Minutes and Marketed Worldwide in Days* (2010).

Another of Burgett's recent general market books was *Niche Publishing: Publishing Profitably Every Time!* (Specifics are available at www.nichepublishing.org).

Burgett has also published 1,700+ articles and offered over 2,000 professional spoken presentations, mostly to associations and conventions and through university extension programs. During that time he has appeared extensively on radio and TV, as a guest author and a publishing specialist. Burgett is a long-standing member of the National Speakers Association, the American Society of Authors and Journalists, and the Independent Book Publishers Association; has produced 26 audio CD and cassette programs, and has written 38 published books, including *Niche Marketing for Writers, Speakers, and Entrepreneurs, Self-Publishing to Tightly-Targeted Markets, Empire-Building by Writing and Speaking, Speaking for Money* (with Mike Frank*), Sell and Resell Your Magazine Articles, Treasure and Scavenger Hunts, Life After Dentistry* (with Dr. Jay Hislop), *Standard Marketing Procedures for Dentists, The Travel Writer's Guide, How to Sell More Than 75% of Your Freelance Writing, The Writer's Guide to Query and Cover Letters, Standard Marketing Procedures for All Dentists* (with Reece Franklin), *Ten Sales from One Article Idea*, and *The Query Book*.

In 2007, three of Gordon's books were revised, updated, and reprinted. These include *How to Plan a Great Second Life*, the *Travel Writer's Guide*, and *Sell and Resell Your Magazine Articles*. His first novel also saw life late that year.

157

Four of Burgett's books have been Writer's Digest Book Club top choices: *Sell and Resell Your Magazine Articles, The Travel Writer's Guide, The Writer's Guide to Query and Cover Letters*, and *How to Sell More Than 75% of Your Freelance Writing*. His *Sell and Resell Your Magazine Articles* was published by Writer's Digest Book Club.

Gordon has owned and directed a publishing company, Communication Unlimited, since 1982. It originally specialized in (and continues to offer) books, reports, and cassettes about writing, empire-building, and niche publishing. For many years it served the dental and medical industry with niche books about standard operating procedures. For the past five years its education imprint has published key books for superintendents, principals, and K-12 teachers, including *What Every Superintendent and Principal Needs to Know, Teachers Change Lives 24/7, The Perfect School,* and *Finding Middle Ground in K-12 Education: Balancing Best Practices and the Law*. (See details at www.superintendents-and-principals.com.)

Burgett earned four academic degrees: B.A., University of Illinois, Champaign-Urbana (Latin American Studies), M.A., University of Wisconsin, Madison (Luso-Brazilian Studies), M.F.T., Thunderbird Graduate School (Foreign Trade), and M.A., Northern Illinois University (History). He was twice a university dean, taught Portuguese and history, created a city recreation program in Illinois, directed CARE (and Peace Corps) programs in Colombia and Ecuador (including the Land Directorship of the HOPE ship medical/dental program in Guayaquil), twice studied in Brazil, played professional baseball, and led a gold hunt up the Paushi Yaco (Upper Amazon) River in Ecuador.

He survived to write newsletters, articles, and books. See his free monthly newsletter at www.gordonburgett.com/nl.htm and his blog at www.blog.gordonburgett.com..

Communication Unlimited
P.O. Box 845
Novato, CA 94948
(800) 563-1454
Gordon@gordonburgett.com

How to Get Your Book Published Free in Minutes
and Marketed Worldwide in Days

Index

How to Get Your Book Published Free in Minutes
and Marketed Worldwide in Days

160

161